A BOOK OF
Pagan Family
Prayers & Rituals

Also by Ceisiwr Serith:

The Big Book of Pagan Prayer and Ritual

A Book of Pagan Prayer

*Deep Ancestors: Practicing the Religion
of the Proto-Indo-Europeans*

Back to the Beginnings: Reinventing Wicca

A Pagan Ritual Prayer Book

A BOOK OF
Pagan Family
Prayers & Rituals

CEISIWR SERITH

WEISER
BOOKS

This edition first published in 2022 by Weiser Books, an imprint of

Red Wheel/Weiser, LLC

With offices at:

65 Parker Street, Suite 7
Newburyport, MA 01950
www.redwheelweiser.com

ISBN: 978-1-57863-771-3

Library of Congress Cataloging-in-Publication Data available upon request.

Cover design by Kathryn Sky-Peck
Interior by Steve Amarillo/Urban Design LLC
Typeset in Arno Pro and Barlow

Printed in the United States of America
IBI
10 9 8 7 6 5 4 3 2 1

For Debbie and Elizabeth.

Contents

Acknowledgments

Many people helped this book along its way. The reference section gives the names of some of them. Special thanks are due to Beth Goldstein, who was the one who said: "You should write a book." John Yohalem, editor of *Enchanté*, made many good suggestions regarding chapter 3. The EarthSpirit Community provided support and guidance, as well as teaching me much of what I know about ritual. I learned more by writing rituals for Ár nDríaocht Féin (especially Nemos Ognios/ Grove of the Living Flame) and by giving presentations at various Pagan festivals.

And, of course, my wife and daughter were vital to this book's creation. They proofread, made suggestions, taught me about family dynamics, and put up with my clumsy early efforts at constructing rituals. My daughter taught me how to make God's Eyes and made sure my directions were correct. I am grateful to all of these people. Any errors or awkwardness found here, however, are my own.

Preface

Around twenty-five years ago, I was telling a friend about the Pagan activities I was doing in my home with my family. She said: "You should write a book." I laughed it off. But her comment started me thinking about what it means to raise Pagan children and to practice Paganism with them in a Pagan home in the modern world.

As I considered how I was handling these issues in my own life, I realized that the problems facing my own family weren't unique. As young Pagans leave their adolescent years behind and begin to raise children of their own, these problems become even more acute. Are we to remain a religion of converts? Or will we be able to develop an organic form of Neo-Paganism that can serve our children—one that will be as much a part of them as their names, one that will grow within them when we are no longer there to feed it? The answers to these questions are at least two generations away. New cultures take time and we won't know whether our efforts have been successful until our grandchildren are grown.

This book is the result of my own attempts to answer these questions. It is primarily a book for families with children. These aren't the only kind of families, of course, but there are already many books that can be used by families composed solely of adults. The kind of Paganism that works with adults doesn't necessarily work with children, however. A different kind of Paganism is required for the young, and that's what I've concentrated on here. For the purposes of this book, I define a family as a multigenerational group, one or more of whom are children, living together and possessing a close tie of blood and/or love.

It can be a hard thing to raise Pagan children in our culture, and we can certainly use all the help we can get. So I invite those Pagans who don't have children to help those of us who do. When our children reach their difficult teenage years—and don't be under the illusion that Pagan children will somehow have an easy adolescence—they will need adults other than their parents to confide in and ask for advice. As Pagans, we all have children. Our children belong to the People, and that makes the next generation everyone's business.

This isn't just a book of rituals and information. Here you will find opinions, arguments, and suggestions. You will probably disagree with some of them. Indeed, your vision of Paganism may be very different from mine. There is no Neo-Pagan authority that hands down final judgments or imposes liturgy. If your views differ from mine, please add your voice to the discussion. The Paganism of the future will have many roots from which a living tradition for the next generation and then the next will grow. After that, they're on their own.

Although I intended to provide a complete system of Family Paganism, this book is more than that. It's an invitation to Pagans to join in the quest for a form of Paganism that can mean something to our children. For this reason, as well as including rituals for a whole host of occasions, I have also pointed the way towards developing your own rituals, both in the text and in the sources and resources. These are as important a part of the book as the set rituals. This is as it should be: Paganism is a tree, not a crystal; it will continue to grow and change as long as earth and sky endure.

The major source I looked to in devising these rituals was the culture of the British Isles. This delightful mix of Celtic, pre-Celtic, Roman, Anglo-Saxon, Norse, Christian, and who knows what other traditions isn't only the source for most of Neo-Paganism. It's also a perfect example of just how effective syncretism can be. Since most Americans have at least some ancestors from the British Isles (or from their cousins in the Germanic and Celtic regions of northern Europe), and since so much of American culture is already based on these cultures, much of this material may seem familiar to you.

This book also draws heavily on the Roman tradition. Roman religion and folk customs are particularly well-documented and present a virtually complete Indo-European Pagan culture. (The Indo-Europeans are a group of peoples with related languages and cultures that include most of those from Iceland to India: the Celts, Germanics, Romans, Balts, Slavs, Greeks, and Vedic Indians, among others.) The Indo-European traditions were especially useful to me in developing rituals for the home and its guardians, as well as for setting the tone for many of the other rituals.

Much of Roman religion took place in the home and is thus especially relevant here. In typical Pagan fashion, what Romans *did* was more important to them than what they *believed*. Indeed, they kept up numerous traditions and practices even though they didn't understand the reasons behind them. The Romans knew how to remember and they have left their mark on Western popular culture. Roman influence has already entered Neo-Paganism through Wicca, both directly—through the classical educations of its founders—and indirectly—through the effects of Roman culture on British folk custom both during and after the conquest. Thus many Roman customs seem like old friends to us.

Many other cultures, from all the continents of the world, have made their marks on this book as well. I have tried to choose from these traditions with respect and not merely plunder them. If any readers feel their culture has been misrepresented, I apologize in advance and ask that they write and educate me.

Most of the rituals presented here can be performed with a minimum of equipment. The items you use may be as special as a Wiccan athame or a ritual knife. They may be special in a different way, like china used only on holidays. Or they may be ordinary things, made special by virtue of being a part of your everyday life. With the exception of weddings, the dedication of babies, and funerals (which require the usual Wiccan tools), the items needed are likely to be found around your house already or easily acquired—items like bowls, bells, candles, and flowers. Rattles and drums are less common than bowls, perhaps, but they're not rare in Pagan households and they're easy enough to buy or make.

Although the practices presented here are all intended to include children, some parts of them are meant to be performed by adults, particularly words spoken in rituals. When this is the case, I have indicated so in the instructions. I have also indicated when these adults are most appropriately the children's parents, and when other participants or officiants may join in. In most of these rituals, the roles performed by adults can just as well be taken by either men or women. In some cases, however, it seemed that one or the other was more fitting. For instance, it would have been a shame to throw out hundreds, perhaps thousands, of years of tradition surrounding the May Queen, and it seemed only right that a Full Moon ritual should be presided over by a woman, as representative of the moon goddess. Of course, you are invited to adapt any of these rituals to meet the needs of your own families and your own beliefs and lifestyle. The Pagan community is made rich by its inclusion of many types of families and a wide range of customs and practices.

I've learned a lot in the time since writing the first edition of this book, which has allowed me to make what I hope are improvements. I've especially learned more about writing rituals. Also, although the first edition was called *The Pagan Family*, it was in fact limited to the Eclectic Pagan/Wiccan family. I've still concentrated on that tradition, since it's the most common form of modern Paganism. However, with the increase in the number and traditions of Reconstructionist Pagans, I thought it was a good idea to include some material for them. Since the most popular forms of Reconstructionism are Celtic, Germanic, Roman, and Egyptian, those are the traditions I've written for. I hope that both types of Pagans can still use most of the book, making appropriate changes where necessary. Finally, I've had the benefit of reviews and readers' comments, and have listened to them as I thought appropriate.

CHAPTER 1

Introduction to Paganism

Paganism isn't merely a thing of the past. It's survived years of neglect and persecution, and is now returning to life. It's spent a long time hidden away in corners of the world or sleeping beneath a thin blanket of Christianity in the folk customs of country people. But now it's waking up. It's a beautiful day, and Neo-Pagans—those of us who are reviving the old ways—are glad to see it back.

Neo-Paganism is a diverse set of beliefs that draws its inspirations from many cultures. Its practitioners range from people pouring out libations on the beach, to shamans riding their drumbeats to the spirit world, to Wiccans practicing complex rites involving special tools and knowledge, to Reconstructionists poring over ancient texts and modern scholarship in an attempt to revive the worship and beliefs of their ancestors. I cannot speak for the details of all of its forms. These are as varied as the people who practice them. But the spirit of Neo-Paganism—its principles, its attitude toward the world—is something that all Pagans share. And of these I can speak.

This World and the Otherworld

Pagans live in *this* world, recognizing it as sacred. We don't see it as merely a temporary thing, nor as the manifestation of some more sacred realm. For Pagans, there is no other world that is more real and of more value than this one. We're not mere sojourners here, marking time until we can die and go on to a "real" and eternal world. *This* is our world; we belong here and we like it that way. When I walk outside each morning, I feel as if I belong. This is my planet and I am part of it, as surely as my fingers are part of me. The sky is above me; the earth is below me; and I walk in between, accepted and loved.

When I walk in the woods, I feel the individual personalities of each tree and stone. When I walk in the city, I feel the complex patterns of power woven by so many people. Either place, I am at home. This is my planet and these are my people.

Pagans are great workers of ritual. No matter how complex or ornate these rituals may be, however, they're not performed in order to escape from the world. Pagans use ritual to *celebrate* the world and to adjust themselves and their lives so as to harmonize with it. They seek to commune with the gods of this world, who are themselves deeply involved with it. We don't conduct these rituals for distant deities, but for old friends. The material world fills our rituals. We orient our rituals and our lives by it.

The most common symbol used by Wiccan Neo-Pagans is the pentagram, adopted from ceremonial magic. This five-pointed interlaced star is the symbol for a reality formed of the weaving together of the four classical elements (Air, Fire, Water, and Earth) with spirit. Matter and spirit are thus not separate for Pagans, but interdependent. Most Pagan ritual actions are performed clockwise to mimic the motion of the sun and moon in the sky. Offerings to our deities are of everyday items, particularly food and drink.

Don't misunderstand me; Pagans are quite interested in the sacred. But for us, that which is sacred isn't opposed to that which is profane. We may make a space sacred for a ritual, but it's the same space it was before the ritual and it will be the same space after it. It's just that, for a time, we are more aware of the sacredness of the space, more attentive to it. The ritual helps us to remember its sacrality. And "remember" is an important word to us.

Paganism isn't a religion of metaphysical dualism. In the Pagan world, matter isn't opposed to, or even separate from, spirit. The material, the everyday, isn't thought of as being somehow not fitting for religious purposes. The earth and all its delights are as sacred to Pagans as those things that are normally considered "spiritual."

Pagans aren't ethical dualists. Evil doesn't exist as a force or a personality. Many of the disasters that beset us (floods, tornadoes, disease) are disasters only from the human point of view. But the gods have many children, and most aren't human beings. The disease that kills me may be the result of millions of bacteria being allowed to live. This is hard on me and I don't like it, and I certainly have the right to fight the disease, but it isn't evil. It's simply part of the great dance of life and death.

The terrible things that humans do to each other aren't proof of an evil force either. When examined closely, they are seen to be unbalanced forms of very positive things: the aggression that helped win us our place in the world, the sexuality that continues our species, the loyalty to family and community that gives us our strength. It's a terrible thing when such wonderful forces are carried to bad ends. The term "sacrilege" comes to mind. But it isn't evidence of an evil force, nor does it challenge the existence or power of the gods.

Although Pagans place an emphasis on the material world, that doesn't mean that they recognize it as the only world. In fact, there's another world existing in close connection with ours—the Otherworld, the Land of Youth, the Dreamtime, the home of the Ancestors, the Land of Faerie. It's the home of gods and spirits, and the source of numinous power. It sometimes seems far away, but it's actually right here, coexisting with ours. Where else would it be?

Perhaps the greatest mystery of Paganism is that, if the Pagan path is followed with dedication, these two worlds approach each other more closely, until we eventually live in both at once. This is one of the ways a Pagan comes to see the sacredness of our world.

Pagan Spirituality

Perhaps you're thinking, "What does all this sacred world stuff have to do with Paganism? I thought Pagans were simply people who believe in more than one god." Of course we do; it says so right in the dictionary. Pagans don't believe that the infinite variety we see around us can be attributed to the action of one sacred being. There is immense variety on the material level, and we believe there is equally immense variety on the spiritual. For this reason, the numinous beings of Paganism are many. From the spirit of a rock, limited in time and space, to the gods and goddesses of particular traditions and cultures, to ancestral spirits, to family guardians, to power animals—the list of sacred beings recognized by Pagans is practically endless. While not every Pagan would choose to work with all of these, most Pagans would accept their validity.

The major deities of Wicca are the Goddess and the God. They are the Mother and Father of All; from their love new worlds are continually born. The Goddess is the origin of being, the power behind the universe, the bringer into manifestation. Although she goes by many names, the most popular among Neo-Pagans are Diana and Isis. The God is the one who acts, the wielder of power, the one who is the mask that reveals the universe. His most popular name among Neo-Pagans is Cernunnos, "The One with the Antlers," for he is frequently depicted wearing these symbols of masculine power and wildness.

Other Pagans, the Reconstructionists, worship a more diverse group of deities that are usually drawn from one particular ancient culture. But ancient cultures borrowed from each other, and many modern Pagans follow this precedent. It's not unusual to find a primarily Norse Pagan giving honor to Lug, for instance, and Irish, Gaulish, Welsh, and Roman deities all find their place in my family shrine. The functions of each of the deities of Reconstructionsts are more limited than those of the Wiccan God and Goddess, but can still be quite diverse. Odin is a god of inspiration, but also of war; Astarte is a goddess of sexuality, but also a protector of cities; Lug is a god of all skills, but also the source of kingship.

These gods and goddesses are protectors and teachers and, like human parents, they must occasionally discipline their children. In their concern for the world, and for their special devotees, these beings can also serve as a model for our behavior as parents.

The fact that Pagans worship a divine that doesn't exclude the female has caught many people's attention. Although at some theological level, the God of the religions of the West may be said to be without gender, this God has been almost exclusively depicted and conceived of as male. The fact that Neo-Pagans celebrate the masculine and feminine divine equally has a great impact on Pagan family life. Neo-Pagan families usually try to avoid sexual stereotypes, encourage excellence in both sexes, and are inclusive of all sexual orientations.

On the other hand, Pagans recognize essential differences between the sexes. Since their divinities are both male and female, however, these differences aren't seen as differences in worth, but rather in type. We welcome and celebrate these differences.

Everyday Deities

Since this book is written for families, not covens, groves, congregations, or mystics, many of the spiritual beings called upon will come from the lower end of the range, the local spirits that shape our mundane lives. The main inspirations for family Paganism are folk traditions, the everyday customs and the holy day traditions of the common people. Its deities are the comfortably worn-down and worn-in ones of the European peasant—threshold guardians, hearth guardians, spirits of the dead, and spirits of the wild. The Shining Ones have their times, and they will be honored here, but it is the more humble household spirits who are most often called upon by Pagan families. This is true for both Wiccans and Reconstructionists.

The beings of power, the gods, exist on a continuum not only of power but also of space and time. Every place and every moment are filled with them, and they can be found by all who open themselves to them. Sometimes I encounter them externally. I feel a quiver, like a whisper or a breeze that just makes itself known without giving more information. Have you ever felt an itch and not known where it was coming from? Encountering the gods can feel like that—like a cosmic itch.

Sometimes they're inside me. Cernunnos comes with strength when I am weak and with courage when I am scared. He fills me; I am taller and larger and more muscular. Antlers reach up from my head, both drawing me up and weighing me down. He is there, and he helps me. And sometimes the gods are right here in front of me. I see them; I hear them. They are here and they are helping me. I make no apologies for this belief.

Sometimes it's not the gods I feel, but their effects. I'm surrounded by their love when I'm lonely. I'm comforted when I'm troubled. And I'm given help when I need it. The gods are there, in the way of the world, in the living and dying that make up our planet. The wind, the waves, the stones, and the trees all reveal them.

The turning of the seasons reveals the sacred as well. When I see the dying of the year, I mourn with it. This mourning is itself a source of strength, for while I may mourn the death of the year, I will rejoice in its rebirth. All this drama is played out within me.

So when I face my own death, I do it with a little less fear and a little more comfort. I have seen the earth die and be reborn, and I know that I'm indeed part of this earth. I too will be reborn, not because I have an immortal soul that is living innumerable lifetimes to learn its way to godhood—although that might be true, and who am I to say yes or no?—but because this is my home. This is where I was born. I grew from the earth and there is nowhere else I belong. You *can* go home again. In fact, *there's no place else you can go.*

I know I'm a part of all this, a part of the turning and changing that are our world. I live now, I will die then, and the world will go on. I'll have done my part and I pray I'll have done it well. No one else could have done it.

But when I am gone, I will have left an effect behind. Everyone I meet will have been changed by me, just as I was changed by them. I'll have left my mark in everything I've consumed, and everything I've produced, for good or for bad. But nothing I do will have left as great an effect on the world as how I raise my daughter—how she comes to see the world and how she goes on to affect it in turn.

The Pagan Way

Despite these wonderful feelings, Paganism isn't about *feeling*. It's about *doing*. Pagans walk a Pagan path. They align their lives with the seasons and the moons. They treat the planet gently. And they show respect to those who share our world—the minerals, the plants, the animals, the people, the spirits, and the deities. It's for this reason that many Pagans are fond of saying that "Paganism isn't just a religion, it's a way of life." This can come across as snobbery, as if other religions aren't serious enough, but it should be taken literally. Paganism *is* a way of life—or perhaps it would be more correct to say it is a way of living. What do you *do*? That will tell you whether or not you're a Pagan. Watch the world. Learn from it. Learn what you have to do to live in balance with its ways. Listen to the world. Hear its voice. It speaks to you in rhythm.

Go to where Pagans gather and you will feel that rhythm. Listen to the drums. They start spontaneously, all sizes and types, and the rhythm grows and changes. The people dance to them. Listen carefully and you'll hear your own rhythms—heartbeat, breath, sleeping and waking, menstruation, life and death and rebirth. Then turn from your own rhythms. Turn from the rhythms of the drumming and the dancing of the community. Turn to the world about you and feel its rhythms. Live these rhythms—day and night, phases of the moon, seasonal flow.

And in the flow, something will seem right. There, on the edge of your mind, is a tickling of memory, like déjà vu. Does it come from another life? Or is it just part of being human? Something tells you to remember. So you try. *Remember* the stories of your ancestors. *Remember* those who died for you. *Remember* that this world is your home. *Remember*, and things will be okay.

The rituals in this book are here to help you and your children remember. When the old deeds are done, when the old songs are sung, the mind remembers, the body remembers. Do you want to understand Paganism? Do the rituals—and remember.

CHAPTER 2

Pagan Rituals

Ritual is the heart and soul of Paganism. It's the sacred acting through which we celebrate the world and the gods. By taking part in ritual, we not only learn how to live rightly—to perform rituals *is* to live rightly. There are rituals of time, when we do what is most appropriate for a given moment, and rituals of place, when we do what is most appropriate for a given location. By performing these rituals at the right time and at the right place, we act rightly. And Pagans *are* what they *do*.

Some rituals are unlearned. Humanity seems to have an innate genius for developing and elaborating rituals; they spring out of us when the moment calls for them. But if a ritual is to have meaning beyond a small group of people, it must be learned. The symbolic acts of a ritual make up a language that must be understood by those who perform it, and this language has to be learned.

This is one of the reasons why Pagans study the old stories, why we make lists of gods and goddesses and their corresponding attributes and rituals. By doing this, we are teaching ourselves a ritual language we can use to communicate with each other, with nature, and with the sacred.

Family Spirituality

The form and purpose of a ritual are affected by the number and type of people who perform it. Covens frequently concentrate on magic; individuals may spend long periods in meditation; large groups often employ sacred drama. A family, though, is a special case. It's a small group, but some of its members are children. And that changes everything.

Neo-Paganism in America has become almost synonymous with Wicca, the British religion developed in the middle of the last century by Gerald Gardner, Doreen Valiente, and others. In the United States, Wicca is still practiced in private covens, but it's also found in open Pagan communities. These communities draw some of their basic assumptions about ritual and religion from Wicca, and, unfortunately, some of these don't work when children are involved.

Traditional Wicca is a Mystery Religion. As such, some of its rites are performed in secret and rely on mysteries that can be understood only by initiates. It's strongly influenced by ceremonial magic. Wiccan rituals involve a heavy symbolism that has to be learned before the rituals make sense. Wicca grew in small groups of adults and its ritual structure reflects that.

Pagan parents often make the mistake of trying to bring children into Wiccan rituals, or of trying to compose rituals based closely on what is done by a coven. This arises from a misunderstanding of the role of Mystery Religions in culture. In a living Pagan culture, Mystery Religions or secret societies may (or may not) play a role, but they're not the whole story. There are also public rites, folk traditions, and mealtime customs—the list of Pagan practices is a long one. But the rituals that Pagans perform in the home aren't the public rituals, nor are they the mystery rituals.

In pre-Christian days, Pagans lived in Pagan communities. With the advent of Christianity, individual and family rites frequently disappeared, or survived in attenuated and Christianized forms. What showed the most staying power were the practices of the entire community—Christianized and secularized, perhaps, but still recognizably pre-Christian.

Many folk customs are only appropriate for communities. If you're a member of a community of Neo-Pagan families, you are a lucky person indeed. Your children will benefit immeasurably from feeling that they're not total weirdoes, that there are too other Pagan children and that you're not just making all this up. And you'll benefit from this support as well. But most of us struggle along alone. This book was written for these people.

I have, as much as possible, adapted the wider community rituals to the family rituals I give here, regretfully leaving out what couldn't be adapted for families with children. I've also "paganized" or adapted those family traditions that either survived the conversion or were later invented by Christians, but in a Pagan-family friendly form. At times, I've given suggestions for those who live in a wider Neo-Pagan community, but the emphasis of the book remains on those families who are practicing alone.

The rituals in this book have therefore been written with a nuclear family in mind. One or two adults and children—that's the family I had in mind when I wrote them. If your family is larger, that's wonderful. It's especially wonderful if it includes three or more generations. I have included suggestions for stretching the rituals, but in general I've written them for smaller family units. It's easier to adapt that kind of ritual to a larger group than it would be to adapt community rituals to a smaller group. As long as the number of people involved doesn't get much higher than a dozen, these rituals will work.

Adopt, Adapt, Reinterpret

Can you do these rituals another way? Most certainly. If you have a single-parent family, or if your family is part of the LGBTQ community, for instance, you'll have to. In fact, as our society becomes more diverse, these changes become more necessary. This happens in other religions as well. In Judaism, for example, it's traditional for the mother to light the Sabbath candles. If there's no mother present, any adult woman may do it. If there's no adult woman present, then a man may do it. Better that than leaving the candles unlit. This isn't to say that for a man to take a woman's part in a ritual is a breach of tradition. It's part of the tradition itself, and those who do it this way aren't performing second-class rituals. Those who adapt traditions in this way are simply following the old ways. In general, though, it's best to establish a pattern and not vary from it without good reason. Traditions are very important to children; doing things the same way tells them that the world is a safe and dependable place.

There will still be times when you'll have to do things differently, like when a family member is sick. You may wish to assign roles differently than I have in a more permanent way. That is certainly your right. To tell the truth, in my own family, we do some of these rituals differently from the way I present them here—I take the mother's parts in the Full Moon observance, for instance.

Pagans are used to following their instincts when it comes to ritual. Personal intuition isn't only allowed, it's encouraged. Even the strictest of Reconstructionists often find themselves faced with a gap in the evidence that must be filled from a non-ancient source. Families will find themselves doing this as well. As your family develops its identity, personality, and orientation, you may find yourself modifying the rituals you use. This isn't unique to Paganism, of course. Next time you're with a group of Christian friends, ask each of them when they put up their Christmas tree and watch the reactions. (The only correct time, by the way, is Christmas Eve.)

When working with a family, however, there's less room for personal intuition. Bluntly put, no one person has the right to make a major change in a family ritual. Fine-tuning, tweaking, and knob-twiddling are fine. You'll find this especially necessary the first time you do a particular ritual. But a major change in something that has been done before with children will defeat the whole purpose of family worship. What it will teach your children is that the rituals are yours, not theirs. It implies that there's no certainty to the cycles being celebrated, that you don't consider either the rituals or them important enough to respect and honor. Tread carefully when making changes, then.

On the other hand, your children will often make changes of their own, frequently in the middle of a ritual. If these changes aren't in keeping with the spirit of the ritual, you'll have to say nicely that you do things another way. You are the adult; you are the teacher. And one of the things you need to teach is that sometimes we can't let what *we* want to do take precedence over the wishes of others. Make sure that you explain your actions after the ritual is over, though.

Most of the time, the changes will be just fine and should be adopted enthusiastically. They give a ritual meaning for the child who makes them, and the fact that you go along with them shows that their opinions are valued. The very fact that children care to make changes at all is a good sign; it shows that they are making Paganism their own. Traditions that you have yourself grown up with may have a more comfortable feel than ones you find in a book (including this one). Children know when you feel self-conscious about something and will, in turn, feel uncomfortable themselves. Traditions take a while to wear down around the edges. Don't be afraid to adapt customs you're used to, even if they're non-Pagan. While some traditions are religious in origin and form, many others are secular. Some are both. Bells at Christmas, for instance, come from both church bells and sleigh bells. Adopt, adapt, reinterpret. Cultures have always done this, Pagan as well as Judeo-Christian.

In fact, it's a time-honored tradition for religions to borrow customs from each other. For example, Neo-Pagans took jumping over a broomstick at weddings from the Romany, who took it from the peasants of the Netherlands and northern Germany. These borrowed traditions don't stay unchanged, however. The tree borrowed from Pagans by Christians became a Christmas tree. If we now adopt it back in its changed form, we will ourselves change it. That's okay. This kind of cultural overlap only serves to enrich both traditions.

Ritual Words

Rituals can have a variety of structures—dramas, declarations, litanies, dances, prayers—the list is long. The language styles can vary as well—Elizabethan, romantic, blunt, etc. The style a family should use will be based on both personal preference and the maturity of the children involved. Let's face it, no matter how exalted Elizabethan English sounds to you, all it will teach a seven-year-old is that religion is boring. So drop the "thees" and "thous" and expressions like "We do bless you." People just don't talk like that and children just won't listen to it.

Your words don't have to be flat, however. Try rhyming, or, if your rhymes are like mine and keep ending up sounding like greeting cards, use alliteration. That was the original poetic form of English. Or try blank verse. Read the soliloquies of Shakespeare and see how the words fit. Say your words out loud before using them in a ritual. Do they flow smoothly? Do they fit with each other? Are there any words that, when put next to each other, sound stupid? ("The nether lands," for instance.) Are all the sentences in the ritual in the same style? Are they simple enough for your children to understand? Most of all, do they mean what you really want them to mean, with no unintended ambiguity? One of the things I've learned is that, if you try to memorize a prayer and keep making the same mistake when you speak it, the words should be changed to the mistaken ones.

In fact, the spirit of Paganism doesn't require words. You can say them before, during, or after the act that accompanies them, or you can eliminate them altogether. The words in the rituals in this book move me or I wouldn't have written them, but it's the actions that are important. Sometimes our minds seize on words like a life preserver—"Oh good, something I understand." But when this happens, the action may not cut to the heart. Words are good for explanations. Actions are good for rituals. Do the deeds. Do what your ancestors did. Stand in their place.

Some of the rituals in this book have relatively long declarations. Instead of one person speaking them, these could be broken up among family members to allow more participation if your family is large. They can also be put in question-and-answer form to involve family members in more than simply listening to speeches made by parents.

One simple truth about children: they usually don't like to listen to a lot of words. They fidget. They ask questions that have nothing to do with what's going on. They turn their bodies to jelly and slide off their chairs. There are things children *do* like, however. As a Pagan parent, your job will be much easier if you do these things. Okay, you can slip in things you like too, but make a sandwich with the kids' preferences as the bread. Children like celebrations. They like parties, presents, and decorations. They like to do things. The same child that went glassy-eyed at your reading of a speech may gladly read it themselves and feel thrilled about it. Since Paganism is a religion of doing, give your children something to do. Let them carry something, move something, say something. The first time our family celebrated Brigid's Day, our daughter took over the ritual. She took the Brigid's Cross and insisted on saying the words in each room by herself.

Kids also like to sing, and Paganism has lots of songs. I give the names of some recordings and music sites in the resources section at the end of the book, and there are lots of songs available online and on video platforms. Play them, listen to them, and sing them with your children. Songs can keep the power to move long after the tradition they belong to has been left behind. Christmas songs still get to me after almost fifty years as a Pagan. This is the power of song.

Listen to your children. They'll let you know what's working and what isn't. But this listening requires great subtlety. A child may "act cool" about something that really matters to them. They may groan when you start to tell a myth and then be drawn in by it and start asking questions about what happens next. They may complain about having to do a ritual, but remind you if you forget to do it. They may fidget when meditating with you, but then you find them meditating on their own. Watch carefully and see what catches fire. Don't give up after one try.

Ritual Elements

Every ritual performed with children (or with adults) should include both the standard and the special, what Catholics call the Ordinary and the Proper. The standard is the frame that tells participants that a ritual is being done and puts the rest of the ritual in a context appropriate to the religious tradition. This repeated framework tells children that the Pagan way is one of reassurance, that it's as steady as the yearly cycles it celebrates, that we aren't just making it up as we go along. The path may turn, but it always turns back to its beginning.

The special element is the part that conveys the message of a particular ritual. In writing the seasonal rituals for chapter 8, for instance, I tried to devise something for each festival that would be unique to it, something that would capture children's imaginations and make them look forward to the day. By giving your children something special to do, something that tells them that they are a part of a religion of beauty, awe, and fun, you will keep Paganism alive in them.

Other ritual elements include sacred space and time, special clothing and colors, ritual postures and gestures, family altars, and prayers and offerings.

Sacred Space and Time

One of the characteristics that Neo-Paganism has inherited from Wicca is a preoccupation with sacred space. In part, this is a result of the influence of ceremonial magic, in which a sacred space, a "magic circle," is necessary to keep magicians safe from the spirits they've called up. It's this sacred space that's also found in many of the ancient forms of Paganism as well. Romulus, for instance, essentially cast a circle when he was founding Rome. (Okay, so it was a rectangle.) There seems to be a standard human urge to live in meaningful space, to recognize or create a place that's special.

A family practicing Paganism in their home has no need to create sacred space before a ritual, however. The home should already have been made sacred by ritually blessing it. But even more important, a home is made sacred by the very fact that a family lives in it. The daily activities of a family are sacred acts, and they continually consecrate the place where they're performed. The home is a temple, and the family table is an altar. Yet particular parts of a house may be seen as having more sacred power than others, with particular deities dwelling in them or watching over them. I'll talk about these in the next chapter.

Instead of creating sacred space when starting a ritual, family rituals should have a clear starting point in time. After a family is gathered together for a ritual, there is often an awkward moment of waiting. Too often, there are a lot of family members looking at each other and thinking or saying, "Should we begin now?" This isn't such a bad thing. In fact, it's a normal mundane thing, which will only make the beginning of the ritual, with its shift to structure and order, even more transformative. There will be a beginning of the rite, a clear break from this moment, a clear indication that sacred time has begun.

There are many ways to do this. I have found that the best is to use a special sound, one that's used for nothing else. Sounds exist in time in a special way, arising and then dying away. Sound can thus act as a divider between times, dissolving the previous time when it's first made and creating the new time as it fades away. A bell that's used only for rituals works well for this, as do drums, rattles, and gongs.

Another way to create sacred time is to start in darkness and then light candles. Or fill a cup or bowl and pass it around so everyone can drink from it or anoint themselves in a rite of purification. You can use more than one of these methods in one ritual, but be sure to use the same method or combination of methods each time. Pick one and stick with it; the point is to condition yourself and your family to shift into sacred time easily.

It's also important that there be a distinct *end* to sacred time. The same sound that started the ritual can end it. The candles can be blown out (something that children love to do). The cup or bowl used for anointing can be brought outside and poured out as an offering.

Special Clothing and Colors

Wearing special clothing can make a time more sacred as well. This doesn't mean you have to don fancy robes or ritual garb. In fact, that's not really appropriate for the sort of atmosphere a family ritual is meant to evoke. Remember Sunday best? Dressing up for the gods shows respect for them. Add something special to what you already wear. Romans covered their heads when they prayed. Greek ritualists sometimes wore ribbons or garlands on their heads. Pendants work well, or other jewelry. A prayer shawl or a stole can be enough.

Colors can be used for different effects. For some rituals, a particular color clothing may be appropriate. You'll find suggestions for these in Appendix C. Obvious choices are black for the dark of the moon, white for the Full Moon, and the green of newly growing things for May Day. Use your imagination to find something appropriate for each occasion.

Ritual Postures and Gestures

Think about the body positions you take during your rituals. Associating one position with a ritual makes for an easy transition to sacred time. One position that's almost universal is stretching out your hands with the elbow bent up, palms forward. This is so common to use while praying that it's sometimes called the *orans* position, the "praying" position. You can find other examples in pictures of deities and their devotees.

Several of the rituals given here call for the sprinkling of water. This sometimes serves to bless, with the drops of water carrying the blessing to whatever and whomever they touch. Sometimes it serves as an act of purification, a symbolic washing of the area. The sprinkling itself is something that children love to do. They may get overly enthusiastic about it, but that's certainly not a problem.

Dip your sprinkler into a bowl of water and shake it in the direction desired. A bundle of flowers or leaves can be used for this. Flowers that are in season will add to the emphasis of a seasonal celebration. Other possibilities include ribbons or threads tied to a stick, a tea infuser in the shape of a spoon, or a small leafy branch. A rattle can also be used to bless. Think of it as a different kind of asperser, sprinkling sound rather than water.

Family Altars

The main altar for family rituals is the family table—the kitchen or dining room table that's used every day or on special occasions. This is the place where the family gathers, where they eat, and, as such, it is sacred. The ancients knew this. For instance, Plutarch, in *Roman Questions* (question LXIV), tells us that the Romans never left the table empty and suggests that this is because it's a sacred place and that sacred places should never be left empty. For this reason, it's good to leave something on the family table—bread, candlesticks, flowers, a bowl of fruit. But it's more important to keep the family table clean and treat it with respect.

Prayers and Offerings

A form of ritual that's often neglected by Neo-Pagans, but one that's suitable for even the youngest children, is prayer. All the types of prayers familiar from other religions can be used by Pagans, although their content and style may be different. I'll have more to say about this in chapter 6.

Another ritual form frequently neglected by Pagans is the giving of offerings. This formed a major part of both family and personal piety in pre-Christian days. Offerings are prominent in the rituals in this book as well.

One of the most common beliefs about household spirits is that they bring with them a responsibility. These spirits don't just give; they must get as well. In Slavic tradition, for instance, guardian spirits who aren't given sufficient respect are known to bring bad luck to their families. So give offerings to your guardians regularly. They seem to like bread and milk best. Set a place for them at your family table at festivals. Tell them about important events in your lives. Give them full respect.

Reconciling Calendars

If you're a member of a coven or grove, your family and your group activities may conflict. There's only so much time, and you may find it necessary to celebrate with one or the other on the day before or after a festival or moon observance. The question is: Which celebration should take precedence? Do you opt for your family celebration because your family is more important than your group? (If it isn't, you need to reexamine your commitment to your family.) Or do you opt for your group on the grounds that psychic work is more affected by dates than family celebrations are?

Fortunately, many of the seasonal family rituals can be done in the daytime (some should be), while many covens or groves meet at night. Some of the other rituals may be a little trickier, though. If you're the only one in your group with a family, you could hold coven or grove meetings at your home after the children have gone to bed. If there are other parents in the group, you could rotate. You could have a big sleepover with all the group's children, assuming they'll actually go to sleep early enough for you to do your work.

Regardless of any conflicts, there should be at least one day in the year when special attention is paid to your household guardians. If yours are ancestors, honor them on Samhain, or Yule for Germanic Pagans (see chapter 8). Other appropriate dates include the anniversaries of your wedding or engagement, when moving into a new house, on children's birthdays, or on any day that strikes you as a new beginning for your household or its members. The Romans offered their guardian spirits cakes, milk, wine, and flowers each month. If you choose to honor yours this well and this often, I'm sure they won't complain.

With most Reconstructionist groups, the decision is easier. Their group rituals are less of a mystery and can be adapted to allow for the presence of children. Indeed, the rituals in this book can often be adapted to the particular tradition of a Reconstructionist group. This will provide the sense of community I discussed earlier and also bring your family together with other like-minded families.

For many of the occasions in the following chapters, I give several rituals. Some are short and simple, while others are full-blown ceremonies. My intent is to offer you a range of styles and complexity that can be tailored to fit your family, your home, and your tastes. They also show the range of options available to Pagans.

CHAPTER 3

The Sacred Home

A home is a temple. This is true in almost all ancient traditions, and it should be especially true for modern Pagan families. As with other temples, the home is a place where we encounter the sacred. It's worth remembering that Pagans encounter the sacred in the everyday world of the home. This should come as no surprise; after all, Pagans live in the sacred at all times.

A home is more than a temple, though, and it's more than a human construction. It's a living being, a microcosm. It's the world of those who live in it, and it has its spirits, just as the world outside does. Most important, the house has its threshold guardian and hearth guardian. These two spots, together with the household shrine, are the most sacred spots in a house. Each has its rituals.

Threshold Guardians

The threshold is the place where inside meets outside. It's the magic spot, the turning point. Such crossover spots are places of awesome power, and even when thresholds have been worn down by familiarity, they retain this power. Threshold guardians are the spirits who protect against external enemies. It's their job to invite in good and avert evil. In short, they're your watchdog spirits. We see an example of their power in the most famous door guardian, the Roman Janus, who has two faces—he looked both ways. That's the sort of power required of a threshold guardian.

This is why it's customary to perform an act of respect when crossing over the threshold—a reverent touch, a slight bow, a pause, anything to say that you recognize and respect the spirit's presence, to show that you belong there and that they can let you in. Even a negative act can honor. I don't step on my threshold and I've taught my daughter not to do so as well. If it should happen by accident, I give a quick apology to the threshold spirit.

Architecturally, the threshold is the doorsill. Threshold guardians, however, dwell in the doorposts and lintel as well, as these are part of the boundary between one place and another. It's the doorsill that's treated as the altar of the threshold spirits, though, and it's there that rites to them are performed. The doorposts are frequently the site of anointings and blessings, however, and figures of threshold spirits may be put there or next to them, either inside or out. We have a Roman coin with the image of Janus on the top of our inside lintel.

In days past, houses generally had only one door. But even when they had more than one, the threshold spirits were held to inhabit only the main door and their rites were only performed there. If you want to recognize their presence at all your doorways, there's nothing wrong with that, but it's not necessary. In an apartment building, honor the threshold of your apartment, not the building's.

If you envision your threshold guardian as Janus, honor him on January 1, his feast day. I pour out a bottle of Italian wine on and around the threshold before entering my house the first time on New Year's Day. However you envision threshold guardians, a natural day on which to honor them is the anniversary of your moving into the house. Since threshold spirits are also the spirits of beginnings, they should be informed before you make any big changes in the life of your family, including major home repairs.

You can also call upon your threshold guardian each night before going to bed. Go to each door—or, alternatively, each one that you've unlocked during the day (this is a good way to make sure that all your doors are locked)—and draw two short vertical lines over the door knob or deadbolt lock, saying:

> *The blessings of Janus be on this door.*
> *Janus it is who guards our doors.*

If you call upon a different threshold guardian, you can replace the name of Janus with the name of your guardian, or just with the words "our threshold guardian."

Although Thor is mainly a deity of thunder and agriculture, he's also a god of protection and can therefore serve as a good threshold guardian as well. Invoke him, like Janus, when closing up for the night. Drawing a Thor's hammer above the doorknob or deadbolt with one of your fingers, say:

> *Thor, protector of our Cosmos,*
> *protect this little cosmos of our own,*
> *our home.*

Hearth Guardians

The hearth, on the other hand, is the heart and center of the home, the source of heat and life. This isn't always true architecturally, but it's true spiritually. The threshold guardian may be the protector of the household, but in the hearth is the spirit of everything that's worth protecting. Its guardian protects, not by repelling evil, but by broadcasting good. It's the home's main guardian.

Hearth guardians are usually female (male fire deities tend to be concerned with public fires). The best known are the Roman Vesta and the Greek Hestia, but the Celtic Brigid has a hearth-fire association as well. Many cultures have chosen not to personify their hearth guardians, being satisfied to acknowledge their presence without needing to know their specific identity. Indeed, even though the Romans named their hearth goddess, there was no statue in her temple in Rome.

If you wish to name your hearth guardian, but don't feel a closeness to either the Graeco-Roman or Irish traditions, I recommend researching your ethnic heritage to determine if your ancestors had a name you'd like to use. An old form of the word *fire* in an ancestral language can be used. The oldest language of the ancestors for many of us is Proto-Indo-European, from which we can form the name *Westya*. This name is created from the word for a home with a feminine ending added and thus means "She of the Home." It's the root of the Roman name Vesta.

Now, you may be thinking that you don't have a hearth. Most of us today don't have fireplaces. But we still have hearths. In fact, you have more than one. Even if you don't have a fireplace, you have a stove, a furnace, and a water heater. All of these are hearths. Since a home can have only one center, however, you must choose one as the ritual location of your hearth guardian. The stove is best, since that's where food, the fuel of the body's fire, is prepared. Put a candle or oil lamp next to your stove, to be lit when cooking your food, either daily or on special occasions. An oil lamp is best, since, even though it has to be refilled from time to time, it's always standing there, a perpetual flame in a sense.

Figure 1. My own hearth.

Figure 1 shows my own hearth shrine, which stands to the left of my stove. It contains an image of Brigid that I painted, an oil lamp for the presence of Brigid herself, a bowl of water for purification, and another bowl for milk offerings. (There's actually no need for an image; the flame is the deity herself.) When I pray to her there, I first purify myself, and then light the lamp, while I say:

> Burn on our hearth, fire of Brigid,
> source of all that is holy.
> Bless this home
> and all who dwell here.
> Smile on all we own
> and give special care to guests
> that our hospitality may honor you.

Each time I open a new carton of milk, I make an offering, pouring some into the bowl when I say "and give special care to guests." This offering can easily be done by children. Each time you turn on your stove or oven to cook, you can say:

> I cook with the fire of [your hearth guardian's name].

This will keep her presence in your mind and bless your food through her.

Household Guardians

A house has its guardians, but so does each family. These spirits watch over each household and all its members. This is an old concept in Paganism that's found virtually everywhere in the world.

These protective spirits come in many forms. Your family may have taken on a god or goddess you feel especially close to. That's certainly fine. But the household guardians who appear in the following chapters are the homey spirits, the comfortable small ones that guide our everyday lives and that are generally associated with only one family.

And, like hearth and threshold guardians, they are frequently name-less. If you choose to name your family's guardians, don't use the names of known guardians; they're already responsible for more than one family. In Eastern Europe, household guardians are referred to simply as "grandfather" or "grandmother," as a sign of respect for their wisdom and age. Use any term that conveys the same to you—Old Ones, for example.

Just who are these household guardians, and where do they come from? You may have a family totem animal, perhaps taken from a coat of arms. Don't use the power animal of one family member who may happen to practice shamanism, however. Remember: this is a *family* shrine. There are ancestral spirits that have, through time, become associated with your extended family, often with no other explanation than that they're traditional. There may even be spirits that guard over a particular house or part of it, like the barn, stove, and yard spirits of Eastern Europe. There are just too many examples of these to give rit-uals for all of them or to discuss them in depth here, but I will describe several below.

As an example to illustrate what these guardians are like, consider the Roman *lares*. These were originally spirits of places that eventually became household guardians. They (there were almost always two) usually appear as pairs of dancing youths pouring out wine. They were frequently confused with the *penates*, who protected the food supply. The lares were offered incense, fruit, and wine. They shared their fam-ily's lives. They stayed with the family wherever they moved, because they were the spirits of the family, not of the physical house (which often had its own guardians).

Here we have characteristics typical of Pagan household guard-ians—there's more than one of them, they're concerned with food, are offered to regularly, are the guardians of the family as a whole and not just one of its members, and have titles rather than names. Moreover, there's a strong connection between household guardians and ances-tors. In fact, some have suggested that the lares were originally ancestral protectors. In many traditions, they're one and the same, and the cus-toms relating to them are similar in other traditions.

Neo-Pagans also often work with these ancestors, those who lived among us and are now in the sacred realm. As such, they're mediators between us and the spirit world, and also the obvious protectors of the family. They're still interested in us and have one foot in our world and one in the Otherworld. A belief in reincarnation doesn't prevent their influence. The Otherworld is all times and all places, and reborn souls can therefore still be contacted through it.

There are two types of ancestors in Paganism—the ancestors of the culture and our own genetic ancestors. The ancestors of our culture are the founders of the way we live. For instance, for a Pagan living in the United States, George Washington is an ancestor of the culture, even though he has no biological descendants. Our genetic ancestors, on the other hand, lived in the world just as we're living, but are now gone. Neo-Pagans should honor both types of ancestors, either on days put aside for the dead or on days associated with them—birthdays and death days, for instance. Both types can be thought of as "the Ancestors." It's the genetic ancestors, however, who are the most important in Pagan family worship.

Household Shrines

A shrine is a great thing to have in a house. Household shrines hold images of deities, ancestors, and other house guardians and/or represent the sacred organization of the cosmos. Physically, a shrine can be many things, depending on your available space, your creativity, and your need for secrecy. The kitchen's a popular location for a household shrine, because that's where the hearth is usually located. The kitchen is frequently where people gather to talk and work; it's where food is prepared and eaten, and it has counter space that can easily accommodate a shrine. Living rooms or family rooms are also good choices, as are entrance ways where protective spirits can be revered going in and coming out. Find a spot where you won't be knocking things over, but that isn't tucked away in an inconspicuous corner.

A household shrine usually contains an altar. This can be a table or a countertop. It has to be high enough to be used standing up and be in a place where its contents can be left set up all the time. If it's absolutely impossible to leave them there at all times, put them there before using the altar.

The two most common kinds of household shrines are cosmological shrines and devotional shrines.

Cosmological Shrines

A cosmological shrine consists of a symbolic representation of the universe, arranged according to your particular Pagan path. Thus a Wiccan household would have representations of the four elements in their appropriate directions, with a representation of spirit in the center. For instance, there could be a feather or incense burner in the east, a bowl with a candle in the south, a bowl for water in the west, and a bowl of salt or sand in the north, with an oil lamp in the center (see Figure 2). Try to make your shrine pretty in some way. It represents the cosmos, after all, and the cosmos is pretty. In fact, the words "cosmos" and "cosmetic" are related.

Figure 2. A typical Wiccan altar with matching bowls to contain the elements to emphasize the desire for balance in the home, and for aesthetic reasons. The elemental symbols were also chosen for aesthetic reasons: white feathers in the east, a white candle in the south, and white quartz in the north. The whole shrine is therefore white and glass.

To set up a Wiccan shrine, place each element on the altar, starting in the east, saying:

> *We call [element] into our home.*
> *May [element] bless it, and all who dwell in it,*
> *and all who are guests in it.*

Set each element down in its place, putting them in their traditional directions: Air in the east, Fire in the south, Water in the west, and Earth in the north. Then put a fire source—a candle or an oil lamp—in the center, saying:

> *We call spirit into our home,*
> *both active and passive.*

Light the flame, and say:

> *May spirit bless it, and all who dwell in it,*
> *and all who are guests in it.*

Let the flame burn for a while, perhaps while preparing and eating a meal, before blowing it out.

The simplest Indo-European cosmological shrine would be a bowl of water, a fire source, and a bowl for offerings. If you want something more complicated, you might have a representation of the World Tree (an ash or oak branch in a pot or bowl filled with sand or pebbles, for instance) and a bowl filled with water to stand for the Well that feeds the Tree (or for the Well of either Mimir or Nechtan). In the middle you could place a candle or an oil lamp as a symbol of the presence of the deities and as a conduit for your offerings, including prayers.

If possible, set the altar up so that when you perform rituals you'll be facing east, the traditional Indo-European direction of prayer. Begin by putting the bowl of water on the left, the direction of darkness and the below, saying:

> *We establish the Well in our home.*

> *May it provide life and inspiration to all who dwell*
> > *in this home*
> *and all who are guests in it.*

Put the tree on the right, the direction of light and the above, saying:

> *We establish the Tree in our home.*
> *May it support our home as it supports the Cosmos.*
> *May it provide life and power to all who dwell in this home*
> *and all who are guests in it.*

Put the fire in the center, saying:

> *We establish a fire in our home.*
> *May it serve to send our offerings to the Holy Ones*
> *and be a sign of their presence in our home.*
> *May it fill our home with the presence of the sacred.*
> *May it provide blessings to all who dwell in this home*
> *and all who are guests in it.*

Let the flame burn for a while, perhaps while preparing and eating a meal, before blowing it out.

Devotional Shrines

A devotional shrine is one dedicated to divine beings. These shrines hold images of the deities that watch over the family, with offering bowls placed in front of each of them, or with a single bowl for all of them.

Devotions to divine beings are performed at this kind of shrine. For a Wiccan, it can be as simple as a representation of the God and Goddess. It can be two candles—white, silver, or green for the Goddess, and yellow, gold, or black for the God. These can be the moon and sun candles found in chapters 7 and 8. Another possibility would be a cowrie shell to represent the Goddess and a vertically extended stone for the God. It's traditional to put the Goddess image on the left and the God image on the right.

You can also add images of deities that members of your family are dedicated to. If you can't find an appropriate image, you can make a rough statue out of clay. In fact, something you make yourself may actually be more powerful than something "perfect" that you purchase. And remember that many deities have animal or symbolic forms. A horse statue can stand for Rhiannon, or a hammer pendant for Thor. You can also use postcards or laminated pictures stood up in a lump of clay. You can easily find pictures online.

Cosmological and devotional shrines can of course be combined, and often are. Many Wiccan shrines, for example, have representations of the four elements with images of the God and Goddess behind them. The shrine in Figure 2 is an example. Figure 3 shows a Celtic or Germanic shrine that also combines cosmological and devotional elements. Moreover, this shrine isn't purely Celtic or Germanic. It contains the Anglo-Saxon Sunne, the Gaulish Esus, a horse for the Gaulish Epona, and the Russian Chur. This kind of eclecticism was common in ancient Paganism.

Figure 3. Celtic and Germanic shrine that combines cosmological and devotional elements. The World Tree is represented by an oak-stained dowel. Ribbons in two shades of green signify leafy branches, although, since ritual trees were often replaced by a pillar, a dowel can serve by itself. In front of the fire is an offering bowl filled with mead; to its left is a smaller bowl filled with water for purifying.

It's interesting that, although Greek rituals are generally linked with just fire and purifying water, we do have precedents for trees, fire, and sacred wells in Greek sources as well. For instance, on top of the Athenian Acropolis there was a saltwater well, an olive tree, and, of course, altars with fire. This kind of shrine would be fitting for Greek Pagans as well, then.

Devotional shrines can hold images of household guardians as well (see below). Because these guardians are often nameless, the images need not be in human form. Possibilities include masks, drums, generic male and/or female statues, or candles. For ancestral spirits, the most common symbols, used in cultures as different as Rome and Africa, are masks. Through them, the ancestors look upon us, and, if the masks can be worn, we take the ancestors' place by wearing them. Since guardian spirits frequently come in pairs, usually male and female for the mothers and fathers of the family, you may want to use two symbols.

Masks for images are easily made from papier-mâché. Blow up a balloon to the size you want. Make a solution of wallpaper paste and water (follow the directions on the package) in a bowl. Tear strips of newspaper, dredge them through the paste, and put them on the balloon in the shape of a face. Cross the strips in layers until you have the thickness you want—four or five layers will do. You can build up large features from crumpled wads and form a nose by folding a cardboard triangle in two, taping it to the balloon, and applying paper strips over it.

Let the mask dry for a day or two. Then pop the balloon and dry the mask for a few more days. Once it's dry, it can be painted. To make the masks more easily recognizable as ancestors, paint them with symbols of your ethnic background. It's very common for ancestor images to be white, a color commonly used for the dead in many cultures. Cut eye-holes if you're going to wear the mask. If not, you can paint the eyes on. The mask will last longer if it's varnished.

If you want to use a drum for your guardian image, choose a flat one that can hang on the wall over your shrine. Decorate it with feathers, ribbons, stones, shells, or symbols painted on or burned into the frame.

You can use this drum in family rituals or just for family fun. Or you can use it as a signal for the beginning of sacred time. In effect, the sound of the drum becomes the voice of the guardian.

Another image you can use is called a "God's Eye." These can be made in pairs, male and female, by using different colors. Blue is traditional for masculine (the sky) and green for feminine (the earth). See chapter 5 for directions on how to make them.

Even though your children may eventually be founding their own nuclear families, they can still be given images of your household guardians when they move out. This will keep them under the protection of the family even though they may be living away from it. This is especially good for college students, who are living separately from the family, but haven't fully left it.

Keep It Simple

The biggest mistake most people make when creating a shrine is cluttering it up. They start collecting magical tools and images and end up with a shrine that looks like a rummage sale. Keep it simple. If there are particular deities that you relate to, go ahead and put their images there, but don't add every sacred object you can get your hands on.

This isn't just a question of aesthetics. A household shrine should be a place of peace and calm that can radiate them to the whole house. If your shrine is instead a jumble of dust collectors it will just radiate disorder. You may find, however, that, regardless of clutter, something comes to you that *wants* to be put on your shrine. Perhaps you find the perfect goddess statue at a flea market, but your shrine is already crowded. Then you have a decision to make.

You can make another shrine in your home for the new piece. (If the piece appeals mainly to one family member, this is the best choice.) You can replace one of the pieces already in your shrine, perhaps moving it to its own shrine. Perhaps something in your shrine has served its purpose in your family's life and can be given away. Perhaps the shrine can be rearranged to form several smaller shrines in the same area. Or perhaps you will simply decide to live with the clutter.

Whatever you choose to do, this isn't the time for one person's intuition to override the wishes of others. The family altar is a family concern, representing the family as a whole, so decisions regarding it must be made as a family. Making the decision together will involve everyone in the religious life of the family and is therefore a religious act in itself.

Use the shrine as often as possible. Your guardians can give advice and help if you take the time to honor them and ask for it. Whenever there's a crisis in your family life, your shrine should be the first place you go to seek a moment of peace and reflection. Family meetings should start with a visit to the shrine to ask for the influence of the guardians on your discussions.

Household Rituals

Morning is a good time for a ritual at your shrine. In this way, you start your day connecting with the holy. When she was young, I used to put my daughter's school lunches in front of the images on my shrine and ask the guardians to bless them after I said my morning prayer. Morning rituals should be short, since most of us don't usually have the time in the morning for anything long and complicated. If you try to use a long ritual, you'll soon grow tired and stop doing it.

Take a moment of quiet in front of your shrine before beginning. Here's part of the morning prayer I use, which could also make up an entire morning ritual.

> Guardians of our household,
> I do you honor.
> Watch over us today as we go about our affairs.
> Keep us safe and happy and healthy.

If you have a Wiccan cosmological shrine, you can simply touch each elemental symbol, saying:

> May the blessings of [element] be upon me this day.

When you touch the center fire source, say:

> *May the blessings of spirit be upon me this day,*
> *enlivening me and filling me with inspiration.*

If you have images of the Goddess and the God on your shrine, touch the Goddess image and say:

> *May the blessings of the Goddess be upon me this day,*
> *filling me with abundant life.*

Touch the image of the God, and say:

> *May the blessings of the God be upon me this day,*
> *filling me with great power.*

If you have an Indo-European shrine, start your ritual by purifying yourself. Then light the fire source and address your patron deities individually, praising them and asking for their blessings. During the praise, or between it and the asking, make offering(s). Leave the offerings overnight and then put them outside for the land spirits. I use nuts, which I can leave in the bowl until it's full and then put outside. When I do, I say: "To the spirits the leavings."

We don't know much about Egyptian domestic religion, although we know from the Rosetta stone that they existed and used deity images. The rituals performed in their temples can probably be adapted for our use. The Egyptians kept a statue of the deity to whom a temple was dedicated in a special room. Each morning, the room's door was opened and the statue brought out and washed before receiving offerings. At night, the statue was returned to the room and the door closed until the next morning.

An Egyptian morning ritual would be more complicated than a Celtic or Germanic one, but can still be short. Purify yourself and the front of the shrine, either with water or with incense. Open the shrine and bow. Make a prayer of invocation, such as:

> *[Deity name], come into our home,*
> *so we may bless you,*
> *and so you may bless us.*

Bring the statue out and purify it with water or incense. Make offerings—beer and bread are traditional—with a prayer like this one:

> *[Deity name], we offer to you.*
> *We provide you with drink,*
> *We provide you with food,*
> *We provide you with praise.*
> *Be welcome in our midst*
> *and be with us through the day.*

Close the door behind the image and leave it out for the day. At night, purify yourself again, then purify the statue, saying:

> *[Deity name], we thank you for blessing and*
> *   helping us today.*
> *Go now to your rest, until we call to you again tomorrow.*

Purify the shrine, put the statue in it, and then close up the shrine.

Calling a Household Guardian

It may be that your household already has a guardian spirit. Perhaps a particular object in your home has an air about it that says that it's become the dwelling place of a spirit. If you're this fortunate, work with the spirit you have. It's more likely, though, that you'll want to call a new spirit.

Put a rattle or a bowl of water on your family shrine. Gather the family together at your main dining table, everyone who will be expected to be under the protection of the spirits, including animals if they can be brought indoors and will stay with you. If this isn't possible, bring the images to the animals at the end of the ritual to introduce them. One family member holds the images and another an offering of food and drink. Establish sacred time and meditate for a moment or two, synchronizing your breathing. With small children, this can simply be a moment of silence. While still breathing slowly, one adult says:

> *One heart beating,*
> *one body breathing,*
> *one life living,*
> *calls guardian spirits to watch over us,*
> *calls them out of the Great Unknown*
> *here to our home,*
> *here to watch over us.*

To call an ancestral spirit, an adult then says:

> *Reaching out and reaching back*
> *to the time of our Ancestors,*
> *we call to you.*
> *Here we are.*
> *The family goes on*
> *and joins with others*
> *in the weaving that makes the People.*
> *We did not spring out of nothing.*
> *We are neither the beginning nor the end of the chain.*
> *You who have gone before us,*
> *be happy for us.*
> *You are here in our midst.*
> *We do not live our lives separately from you.*
> *We do not forget you.*
> *See, we will keep your images in a place of honor,*
> *in our shrine and in our hearts.*
> *We will not forget you.*
> *Do not forget us.*
> *Watch over us.*
> *Keep us safe.*

Light your hearth deity's lamp and make an offering. Then light the fire in the main shrine from that flame. Put the guardian symbols there. These can also be hung on the wall or supported by stands. Gods' Eyes (see chapter 5) can be displayed stuck into bowls filled with sand or pebbles. An adult says:

> *The images of our ancestors*
> *give form to their spirits*
> *that they may watch over us*
> *and help our daily lives.*
> *What we offer to these images*
> *is given to our ancestors.*
> *They are part of us*
> *and we are part of the chain of lives*
> *from the beginning to the future.*

If it isn't an ancestral spirit you are calling, say:

> *These images will serve as homes to our guardians,*
> *a place for those who watch over us.*
> *What we do in front of these,*
> *we do in front of them.*
> *What we say to these, we say to them.*
> *What we give to these, we give to them.*

The "we . . . to them" may be said by everyone. If you're using a drum, one of the adults holds it up and says:

> *This drum speaks with the voice of the spirits,*
> *the voice of those who watch over us.*

Each family member then bangs on the drum at least once. Then hang it on the wall above the shrine. After the images are installed, introduce all the family members to them. Then offer to the guardians, saying:

We do not only take.
We do not only ask.
We ourselves give.
We give ourselves.
We feed you; you feed us.
We watch over you; you watch over us.
Like strands in the same web, we are.

If you are using a rattle, shake it at the images, then turn and shake it over the head of each family member. Alternatively, the rattle can be passed around and used by each person. If you're using water, sprinkle some on each person.

Blessing a New Home

If you can do this ritual before moving into your new home, so much the better, but it's never too late. The ritual consists of ten parts—blessing the borders, offering to the land, blessing the threshold, cleansing, blessing the hearth, establishing a shrine, invoking the elements, blessing the rooms, sealing the windows and doors, and preparing and eating a ritual meal.

1. **Bless the borders:** If possible, go all around the outside of the home, censing and sprinkling water and/or giving offerings as you go. Be sure not to use salt or saltwater, which can harm plants. If you want to incorporate all four elements, use sand or cornmeal for Earth. Before you circle, say:

   Blessed be this land.
   Our home stands on sacred space.

   As you go around the home, pay attention to your land. Inspect it with ritual awareness. If you can't go around the outside, go around the inside, keeping as close as possible to the walls. In either case, go clockwise, since this is the traditional direction for circumambulating anything sacred.

If you live in an apartment or condominium that has common land, you can circle that. If there's no surrounding or common land, make an imaginary trip around the borders of the building. Start at one corner in your home, and go clockwise around it, describing the outside of the the building, as you go. Include all architectural features—doors, windows, steps, pillars, fire escapes, etc.

If you own land (even just a yard), go around the entire border of it, paying special attention to its corners. You may want to put markers at the corners that you can use as altars for offerings to the spirits of the borders. Stone markers are best because they're permanent, but posts will do. Posts have the advantage of being easy to carve, paint, or otherwise decorate with a face or protective symbols if you wish (see Appendix A). These markers can be naturally shaped stones, but pillars are better because their impression of verticality sets them off from the horizontal ground and says: "Here is a border."

Border markers don't have to be large. A foot high is fine. The important thing is that they be visible, at least to those who know their significance. This shouldn't be a problem if the land is your own, but on common land you may need to go without markers, or use sticks pushed in flush with the ground, small rocks, or features that are already in place. Sometimes builders place concrete markers at the corners of a property when a house is built. Look for these, and use them if they're already there.

Before you erect each marker, pour out some wine and put an egg and grain or bread in the hole where it'll be put. As you do so, say:

We give these gifts to the spirits of the land
who were here before we were.

Though we may now claim this land as ours
it was yours long before
and it will be yours when we are gone.
Do not begrudge us its use
but may there be friendship between yours and ours.

Then erect the marker while saying:

God of the borders, watch over our land.

If you work in the Roman tradition, say "Terminus" instead of "god of the borders." If you're a Greek Pagan, you can address Hermes.

Both the spirits of the land and the god of the borders should be given offerings on special occasions such as the anniversary of your moving into the house or when your household is in need of particular protection. Terminus was honored on Terminalia (February 23, March 1, or the last day of the year). I give a ritual for this day in chapter 7.

In some parts of the British Isles, the borders were honored in the past by entire villages in a custom called "beating the bounds." The villagers would process around the village's borders, and at landmarks or corners children were whipped or ducked in cold water. The explanation given was that this would "help them remember." Similar rituals were held in Greece, Rome, Russia, Norway, and other parts of Europe. Now, I'm not suggesting that you whip your children, but they could be the ones to put out the yearly offerings.

2. **Offer to the land**: Tour your yard, paying special attention to any outstanding natural features—large rocks, streams, small hills, etc. Say hello to each tree and leave a small offering of food and drink. If there are too many to do this individually, do it at each group of features.

3. **Bless the threshold**: Bless the main threshold of the house before entering for the rest of the ritual. If you want to bless the other thresholds as well, do so, but without the offering to the threshold guardian. Bless the threshold with the elements and leave an offering beside it, or even pour out a whole bottle of wine or beer on it. If you pour correctly, the liquid will go outside rather than inside. Most thresholds in new houses have a lip to help seal the door when it's closed. As you offer, say:

> Watcher of the threshold
> who looks both ways
> who guards coming in
> who guards going out
> watch over our family and all of our guests.
> Guard our coming in
> guard our going out.
> Open onto a home filled with love and peace
> and hospitality for all guests.

If this is your first home, add:

> God of all beginnings,
> look with special favor on this,
> our first home.

If you work in the Roman tradition, say "Janus Pater" before the prayers. If you use an image of a threshold guardian, install it near the main door.

4. **Cleanse**: It's an unfortunate fact that many of the things that have happened in your new home before you move in might not have been pleasant. Unpleasant happenings leave their traces behind and could cause problems if allowed to stay. The first thing that should be done after entering, then, is to clean. An actual physical cleaning is a good idea, especially

vacuuming and sweeping, both wonderful ways to banish. If you concentrate on banishing undesired influences while you clean, it will be especially effective. After the cleaning, take your noisemakers—your bells, rattles, drums, and horns; if you have a drum for your household guardian, definitely use it. Make as much noise as possible while shouting:

Everything that is bad
everything that could hurt
go away,
Get out!

Ritually, noise is said to disturb harmful spirits. Psychologically, it acts as a catharsis, and the following silence seems peaceful in comparison. (And children love it.) Repeat the last two lines as many times as you feel necessary.

5. **Bless the Hearth**: If you're lucky enough to have a fireplace, light a small fire in it, saying:

The heart of our home is burning brightly.

Give the hearth offerings, especially of incense, cooking oil, or butter (preferably clarified), saying:

Queen of the hearth, be here in our home.
Warm it and light it.
Keep love's flames high.

If you use a Brigid's Cross (see chapter 8), hang it over the mantle. Using a taper, carry fire from the flame in your fireplace to light your hearth lamp or candle (or light the hearth lamp now), saying:

The fire of [name of your hearth goddess] is the flame
on our hearth,

the fire of [name of your hearth goddess] is the flame
in our hearts.

You can light incense from this fire source at this point,
especially if you haven't been able to offer to a fireplace
before. Leave the fire(s) burning throughout the rest of the
ritual.

6. *Establish a shrine*: Set up your household shrine and leave
offerings of bread and salt. If you're establishing a new
household after starting a new family, perform the ritual to
attract a household guardian (see above).

7. *Invoke the elements*: On the altar of your shrine, put the
symbols of the elements as described above. Raise the
image of each element up in turn, beginning with Air, and
turn clockwise around to present the element to the house
while you or another adult says:

> *We bless this house by Air—*
> *the breaths of song,*
> *the breaths of talking with friends,*
> *the slow breaths of meditation and prayer,*
> *and the quiet breaths of sleep.*
> *By Air be clean.*
> *Be fresh.*
> *Be pure.*

Raise the symbol or image for Fire, while you or another
adult says:

> *We bless this house by Fire—*
> *the fire that will warm it,*
> *the fire that will cook our food,*
> *the fire that burns within us,*
> *the fire of life and love.*
> *By Fire be clean.*

Be fresh.
Be pure.

Raise the image or symbol for Water, while you or
another adult says:

We bless this house by Water—
all that we will drink,
all that we will cook with,
all that we will clean ourselves with,
the very blood that runs through our veins.
By Water be clean.
Be fresh.
Be pure.

Raise the image or symbol for Earth, while you or another
adult says:

We bless this house by Earth—
from which it springs,
on which it rests.
We are creatures of earth,
Living upon it,
Living from it,
Living within it.
By Earth be clean,
Be fresh,
Be pure.

Finally, raise the image or symbol for spirit, while you or
another adult says:

We bless this house by Spirit,
by active and passive we bless it.
The Spirit that sustains us,

wrapping around us,
keeping us safe in its arms.
By Spirit be clean
Be fresh
Be pure.

Children can do the presenting, and older children can say the words with everyone else joining in with: "Be clean, be fresh, be pure."

After the rest of your shrine is in place, install any patron deities you may have, naming them as you do so, saying with each:

[Name], watch over this home,
and all who dwell in it,
and all our guests.

8. **Bless the rooms**: Mix some salt with the water and light the incense from the candle. You now have consecrated water that combines the two female elements (Earth and Water), and burning incense that combines the two male elements (Air and Fire). Use these to bless the house, sprinkling and censing as you go. Quite young children can do the sprinkling, while slightly older children can do the censing.

Go through the house, cleansing and blessing each room as you come to it by sprinkling, censing, and saying a short prayer. Suit the prayer to the room and the function it will perform. For example:

May this kitchen be blessed
that all the food prepared in it
will give not only nourishment
but pleasure.

May this bathroom be blessed,
a place of cleaning and health,
that all who use it may be refreshed.

May this bedroom be blessed,
so that it might give peace and rest
to all who sleep in it.

May this guest room be blessed.
May it help us to fulfill our duties as hosts
and bring blessings to our guests.

May this living room be blessed
that it may be a place of fun and relaxation
for all who use it.

May this storage room be blessed
that it may keep in safety
the goods that are entrusted to it.

9. **Seal the windows and doors**: Go to each window, door, or other opening (chimney, dryer vent, etc.) and draw a symbol of protection over it with an athame, a wand, or your hand (see Appendix A). This can be done as you come to them while you are censing and sprinkling. As you draw the symbol say:

   This opening is sealed,
   guarded against all that would harm.

10. **Eat a ritual meal**: Finally, prepare and eat a meal. Use your best place settings and one of the meal prayers given in chapter 6. The food should include bread (that you may never hunger) and salt (that your life may always have flavor). The bread and salt really should be given to you by someone welcoming you

to the neighborhood, but you'll probably have to improvise. Don't forget to provide them for others, though, when *they* move in. You can explain it as an old custom (which it is). It's most common in Eastern Europe, but the combination of bread and salt is found in many cultures, among the Romans and the Irish, for instance. Many Americans are familiar with it from the movie *It's a Wonderful Life*, in which someone is welcomed to a new home in this way.

Moving Out of a Home

Right from the beginning of living in a new home, you'll want to have a proper relationship with it. You want it to become sacred space, so that your living in it will be a sacred act. Remember that moving into a new home means moving out of an old one. In the excitement of moving, don't forget to close off your ties to the home you're leaving.

If your stay in your old home was pleasant, you'll want to bring as many positive influences with you to your new home as possible. Walk through the old house, the whole family together, and remember what's happened there. When you're finished, say:

> We will hold these things in our hearts
> and they will always stay with us
> even as we go on to new places and ways.
> Spirits of this place,
> We invite you to come with us.
> May there be peace between us always.

When you pack, leave your household shrine until the last. As the soul of your home, it needs to remain there as long as it's your home. Make sure the movers know it's to be left alone. Before you pack it away, explain what's happening to your household guardians. They should have been told already, but you need to do it again as part of the leaving ritual. Bring the items in your shrine with you in a box as you travel to your new home.

Of course, if there are influences you don't want to bring with you, you should do things differently. You might even consider disposing of your shrine and establishing a completely new one at your new home. At the very least, purify your shrine's objects the way you would purify new ones. Leave them outside in the sun or rain, or bury them in salt for a day or two. Dispose of the salt afterward; don't use it for anything else. After purifying the objects, bless them again. If there are other objects that appear to be the center of bad influences, like gifts from disruptive people or items in rooms where arguments were frequently held, abandon or purify them as well.

Other Household Rituals

The Romans worshipped a goddess of sewers named Cloacina. If you work in the Roman tradition, or if, like me, you just think it's cool to have a goddess to watch over your plumbing, offer to her from time to time, at least once a year. Pour Italian wine down one of your drains while saying:

> *Cloacina, we call you here.*
> *Cloacina, who provides clean water,*
> *Cloacina, who takes dirty water away to be purified:*
> *bless this home, and all who dwell in it, and all our guests.*
> *May we be healthy, free from illness.*
> *Cloacina, accept our prayer and our offering.*

If you're calling to this or a similar goddess, do so between blessing your hearth and establishing your shrine. You can dispose of leftover liquid offerings by pouring them down the drain, while you say:

> *To Cloacina the leavings.*

At least once a year, give Cloacina her own offering.

If you're working in a northern Indo-European tradition, leave out the elemental section given above and instead install your well, fire, and tree. Put the well in place, saying:

> *We establish this home in the world below.*
> *May it and all who dwell in it,*
> *and all our guests,*
> *be well-supported,*
> *and may they receive inspiration when they ask for it.*

Put the tree in place, saying:

> *We establish this home in the world above.*
> *May brightness shine down on it,*
> *and on all who dwell in it,*
> *and all our guests,*
> *that they might be blessed by the Celestial Ones.*

Put the fire between them and light it from your hearth fire, saying:

> *We establish this home in the world about us.*
> *May it be well-centered,*
> *and all who dwell in it,*
> *and all our guests,*
> *that they might always be surrounded by the sacred.*

As soon as possible after the house blessing, have a housewarming party. One of the responsibilities of a householder is hospitality. It's also one of the joys.

CHAPTER 4

New Life and
New Beginnings

It's my belief that children are born religiously pure. No matter what this little soul's karma may be, in this incarnation they are without flaw. This condition continues until they're old enough to make their own mistakes. It was this attitude that allowed Sioux children to wander unchecked through the most sacred of ceremonies—the sacred cannot be disturbed by the sacred.

The point of rituals performed for children, then, is not to purify them, but to incorporate them into the family and the community, and extend the protection of the gods and the household guardians over them. As soon as family members see a new child, whether it's born into the family or adopted, each family member say:

> *Little One, welcome to our family.*
> *We have waited so long to see your face*
> *and sing to you our welcoming songs.*

All members of the family should do this, including other children who are old enough. Children too young to say the words can just give a hug or kiss instead.

After the birth it's appropriate for the mother to make a special offering or prayer of thanksgiving to any birth or mother goddess to whom she has prayed for help during pregnancy. Suitable offerings include bread, cookies, eggs, milk, flowers, and sandalwood, rose, or mint incense. When offering, this prayer can be used:

> *Goddess of Mothers,*
> *We have been pregnant together*
> *and now I, like you, have given birth.*
> *Thank you for bringing me through this time*
> *and for helping me to deliver a beautiful child.*

Oddly enough, to some of the ancient Pagans at least one of the goddesses who presided over birth was a virgin. For instance, in Greece this responsibility was given to Artemis. If the mother has prayed to a virgin deity during pregnancy, she would, of course, leave out the second and third lines, and replace the first with an invocation to that particular deity.

Blessing and Presenting a New Child

In the miniseries *Roots*, a father presents his newborn child to the earth and sky. This delightful custom wasn't the invention of a screenwriter, however. Nor is it found only in Africa. It was also common among Indo-Europeans and the Japanese. The meaning is clear: the child belongs to earth and sky, and they are being brought before them for the earth and sky's acknowledgment and blessing. This can be seen as presenting them to the God and Goddess if the family is Wiccan, or if they're not, as presenting the child to the whole world (earth and sky together).

When a new child arrives—in the case of childbirth, as soon as the mother feels up to it—take the baby outdoors and place it on the ground. (If there's snow on the ground, put a blanket down first, or perform this part of the ritual indoors using a bowl of dirt.) The mother, or one of the parents, begins by saying:

> *Born of earth.*
> *The Mother [or Earth] knows Her children.*

The father, or the other parent, should then pick up the child and hold them up to the sky, saying:

> *Conceived under the sky.*
> *The sky knows its children.*

This moment can be quite powerful, giving the parents an occasion to ritually acknowledge their new responsibilities. One or both of them then say:

> *You are the child of earth and sky*
> *and you will live your life between them,*
> *Mother and Father to you*
> *and to all living things.*

Some people plant a tree when a new child arrives. If you can be relatively sure you'll be living in the same place when the child is grown, this is a lovely custom. Be careful, though; the fate of your child may be bound with that of the tree. If the child was born to you, you may wish to dispose of the afterbirth or umbilical cord ritually by burying it as you plant the tree. This will tie the child to the place even more, so consider carefully if you want to do this.

Introducing to the Household Guardians

Although it may be assumed that the spirits of the household, like the parents themselves, have learned to know and love the child during the pregnancy, a new child must still be presented to them in order to inaugurate a ritual relationship with them.

As you bring the child across the borders of your property, make an offering of eggs, flowers, wine, or grain to your border guardian, saying:

> *Crossing your border is one of your own.*
> *See this child, know this child, remember this child.*
> *Protect this child's property.*

Then go to the house, place the child on the threshold, and say:

> *Guardian of the Threshold,*
> *Here is one of us.*
> *A new member of our family has come home.*
> *Remember this child.*
> *Watch over this child's comings in.*
> *Watch over this child's goings out.*

Touch a cup of water, milk, or wine to the child's lips, and sprinkle some of it on the threshold. Take the child to the household shrine and say:

> *Guardians of our household,*
> *Here is one of us.*
> *A new member of our family has come home.*
> *Remember this child.*
> *Watch over this child as he/she goes about his/her*
> *daily affairs.*
> *Keep this child safe.*
> *Keep this child happy.*
> *Keep this child healthy.*

Again touch the cup to the child's lips and hold the cup up in offering to the guardians. Then place the cup in front of the guardian images and leave it overnight. In the morning, offer the rest to the spirits of the wild.

Naming a Child

After a baby has been introduced to earth and sky and presented to the household guardians, there's still one more ritual that should be performed, that is officially giving them their name. Having taken their place in the family, they are now presented to the larger community. Naming should take place after the remainder of the umbilical cord drops off. Until then the baby is still connected spiritually to their mother in a way that they aren't to others.

Since a name is what a baby is called by others, and since relatives may well expect a celebration (and they have a right to do so, since a baby is an addition to the whole family), this is best done with your extended family and friends. This ritual is commonly called "saining" by Neo-Pagans. The term, which derives from a northern English dialect, is simply that dialect's version of "signing," referring to making the sign of the cross over the child. It was thus a term for Christian baptism. Because of this, some Pagans avoid using the term, while others have no more hesitation using it than Christians had adopting the originally Pagan "Easter" for their most holy day.

There's no uniquely Pagan way to choose a name for your child. Some Pagan cultures have chosen names that refer to events surrounding a child's conception or birth. Others have sought a name through divination. An interesting variant on this is the custom found in both Wales and Ireland of naming a child based on a chance remark made after its birth. Still others have used family names, names that reflect the order or day of birth, or simply names the parents like. Most of the names that are common in your culture are fine.

Many Pagans like to name their children after Pagan heroes or gods. This is fine, although it might be best to avoid the names of the higher gods. Ancient Pagans who included gods in their names usually used such compounds as "Mithra's friend," or "Servant of Lug." Using unmodified gods' names for children has generally been a sign that the gods are no longer believed in. Naming a child after a god you believed in was interpreted as what the Greeks called hubris—a claim to equality with divinity.

Children can also be named after ancestors. Boys are often named after their fathers' people, while girls are often named after their mothers'. My personal preference is for all children to have a name of their own, so they'll have their *own* deeds to live up to.

Please don't choose a name that's difficult to spell or pronounce, or one that's spelled in an unconventional way. You'll be condemning your child to a lifetime of misspelling and/or mispronunciation. My legal last name is slightly different from a more common one, and I've had this problem my whole life. It's not much fun.

Divining to Choose a Name

If you've narrowed down the choice of possible names to a small number without any one becoming the obvious choice, you can choose one through divination. This can be done simply by writing the names you're considering on pieces of paper or tiles and then drawing one blindly from a bowl. Before drawing the name, say:

> *Lady and Lord,*
> *Divine Parents,*
> *You have given us a child.*
> *Now help us choose a name.*

For non-Wiccan parents, replace the first two lines with either the names of your family's patron deities, with the deity you hope will become the child's patron deity, or with a deity or deities of childbirth or childhood. If you don't know the sex of the child yet, you'll have to do this twice, of course.

Dedicating a Child

The main purpose of a dedication ritual is to name the child. Its secondary purpose is to place the child under the protection of the deities. This is a natural desire; childhood is almost universally seen as a dangerous time and children need all the help they can get. It's also natural to want your children to grow up with the same worldview and morals as you. Children need guidance in this, and what other spiritual path are parents more qualified to teach than the one they're on themselves?

To help the parents in this task, and to ensure that the child is seen as the responsibility of the community, the ritual given below appoints godparents. They are called "guardians" in the ritual to avoid confusion with Christian baptism, although that may also be an awkward term because it can be confused with the concept of a legal guardian. If you want to use "guardian" in the ritual itself, though, "godparents" might be just the word to use when you're explaining the position to non-Pagans.

The ritual I give here is written to be done by more than just the immediate family. If at all possible, that's how it should be performed. The child is being welcomed into the world, and the world is not just the immediate family. It may therefore be performed in the presence of understanding non-Pagans, but please brief them beforehand. Inviting someone to a "baptism" that turns out to be Pagan rather than Christian would not be a good introduction to Paganism. This ritual calls for representatives of the elements as well as guardians. Older children can serve in this role. This is also a nice way to incorporate extended family or friends.

It may be impossible to perform this ritual as written, since not all Pagans know other Pagans who can take part. It can, however, be done by fewer people, or even by the parents alone. My wife and I did it that way ourselves when we were living in England, thousands of miles away from our families and friends. Simply remove the challenges to the parents and guardians and drop the passing around of the child. Then the parents take the roles of priest and priestess, and step in as the representatives of the elements. Instead of one person speaking these words, have the parents speak them together or alternately.

The declarations of what it means to be a parent or a guardian are based on my own understanding of these responsibilities. If your understanding is different, rewrite these words to reflect your own beliefs and the needs of your family. Since these are essentially oaths, they should be written beforehand rather than made up on the spot. The parents and guardians are binding themselves to the child and to their responsibilities toward them. They aren't expressing themselves here; they're swearing their willingness to step into roles that have existed since sexual reproduction has.

Wiccan Dedication Ritual

If you are dedicating a child to the Wiccan path, the ritual will be built around invocations of the elements. Because this ritual is attended by people who are not in the immediate family, it will sometimes be held outside the home. If so, you'll need to create sacred space by casting a circle, or whatever means your tradition uses. Put a table in the middle of the circle and put on it whatever you'll need for establishing sacred space, along with water, olive or corn oil, and milk. The representatives of the elements go to their respective directions, holding symbols of their elements. If the child is a girl, a priest presides; if the child is a boy, a priestess presides. The example given here is written for a female child and with you as one of the parents; if it's being done for a boy, replace "she" with "he," and "her" with "him" as appropriate. If you're a single parent, adjust the words accordingly.

Create your sacred space as usual, then call the directions.

> *Spirits of the East*
> *Spirits of Air*
> *A new child has been born to us.*
> *Come to see her.*
> *Come to bless her.*
> *Come to us who wait for you.*
>
> *Spirits of the South*
> *Spirits of Fire*
> *A new child has been born to us.*
> *Come to see her.*
> *Come to bless her.*
> *Come to us who wait for you.*

Spirits of the West
Spirits of Water
A new child has been born to us.
Come to see her.
Come to bless her.
Come to us who wait for you.

Spirits of the North
Spirits of Earth
A new child has been born to us.
Come to see her.
Come to bless her.
Come to us who wait for you.

Call on a mother goddess from your tradition—Danu, Demeter, Isis, etc.—and call on a father god—Woden, Zeus, etc. For instance, you can say:

Danu, Our Mother
We ask your presence here
to bless this child we bring before you.

Since this is given as a ceremony for a female child, the Priest says:

We meet today to bless this child, to place her on the path to
happiness, and to name her. Naming is no slight thing,
for it is said that the name is the thing. The path is no
slight thing, for of the many that she will find, perhaps
there is only one path that will lead her to happiness.
And let no one disparage the blessing of the gods, the
protection of the elements, and the love of the People.
You who come before us, who are you?

The parents answer:

[Their names], parents of this child.

The priest then challenges the parents, saying:

> *Do you know what it is to be a parent?*

The parents reply:

> *It is to love and nurture,*
> *to watch a child grow*
> *and lead her to the path to right living*
> *that she may know the good*
> *and, knowing it, choose it.*
> *It is to teach and to learn.*
> *It is a way of great joy and great pain.*
> *It is to take in and cherish so that one day you might let go.*
> *It is the greatest responsibility we can take:*
> *For our love has become manifest in a person*
> *and who may know its end?*

The priest responds:

> *You answer well. May all the gods,*
> *who give birth to the world,*
> *guide you in your responsibilities.*

The priestess then challenges the child's guardians, saying:

> *You who stand here with these parents, who are you?*

The guardians answer:

> *[Their names], chosen to be guardians for this child.*

The priestess asks:

> *Do you know what it is to be a guardian?*

The guardians answer:

>*It is to open the many paths before a child,*
>*to show her the ways she may take,*
>*to help her choose that which is hers,*
>*and, once she is on it, to help her live by it.*
>*It is to be second parents,*
>*ready to counsel, ready to love,*
>*always to be there when needed.*

The priestess says:

>*You answer well.*
>*May all the gods, who give birth to the world,*
>*guide you in your responsibilities.*

The parents then place the child on the altar, where the priest traces a pentagram or other symbol of blessing on her forehead with water, saying:

>*May all the Holy Ones keep this child pure.*
>*Let all that is wrong be far from her.*

The parents then take the child to the east, where a representative of the Spirit of Air blesses her by censing, blowing, waving a fan, or ringing a bell, saying:

>*Little one, receive the blessing of Air.*
>*Keep, as long as you can, your holy innocence.*
>*Greet each day joyously,*
>*Always rejoicing in its newness.*
>*Greetings from the Spirit of Air,*
>*Your protector and friend.*

The parents then go clockwise to the other quarters. At the south, the child is passed over the candle flame (be careful of long garments), while the representative of the Spirit of Fire says:

> *Little one, receive the blessing of Fire.*
> *Receive the creative spark to dream with,*
> *the courage to keep your ideals,*
> *and the will to make your dreams come true.*
> *Greetings from the Spirit of Fire,*
> *Your protector and friend.*

At the west, the child is sprinkled with water, while the representative of the Spirit of Water says:

> *Little one, receive the blessing of water,*
> *the womb from which we all come.*
> *Yield gracefully to what must be,*
> *knowing the treasures you hold within.*
> *Greetings from the Spirit of Water,*
> *Your protector and friend.*

At the north, the child is sprinkled with salt or sand, while the representative of the Spirit of Earth says:

> *Little one, receive the blessing of Earth,*
> *the earth from which you grew.*
> *Be strong in silence and fertile in growth.*
> *The North is darkness, out of which comes light.*
> *Greetings from the Spirit of Earth,*
> *Your protector and friend.*

The child is then laid on the ground in the center of the circle. If you're inside, or if the ground's too cold, touch the child's feet to dirt in a bowl. While this is done, the mother, or one of the parents, says:

> *Receive the blessings of the Earth:*
> *May She protect you all of your days,*
> *wrapping Her arms around you as you go your way.*

The father, or the other parent, holds the child up to the sky and says:

> Receive the blessings of the Sky:
> May he protect you all of your days,
> watching over you as you go your way.

The parents then hold the child in the center of the circle, while the priest traces a protective symbol over her, saying:

> Little one, receive the blessings of Spirit,
> which binds the four together,
> from which they are formed,
> and through which they are made manifest.
> The Spirit is your home;
> Be open to it, both gentle and vigorous:
> Return to the center in times of trouble.

The parents carry the child to the altar, where the priest puts a drop of milk in her mouth, saying:

> May you always have plenty.

The priest puts a drop of wine in the child's mouth, saying:

> May you always be happy.

The priest puts a drop of water in the child's mouth, saying:

> May you always be pure.

The priestess then traces a protective symbol with oil on the child's breast, saying:

> Little one, you are [child's name],
> This will be your name until the time comes
> when you are admitted to full worship before the gods.
> Bear it well, and may you do it honor.

The priest and priestess then whisper into the child's ears so only they and she can hear a secret name that the parents have chosen. This is a name that the parents can use when calling on the gods for the child. After being told the name at a suitable age, she can also use it herself in this way.

The priest then stretches out his hands over the baby and says:

> *May all the gods smile gently upon you.*
> *May you choose your path wisely*
> *and walk it well.*
> *May you be gentle and strong.*
> *May you be loving and wise.*
> *And may you be happy,*
> *for the world is good.*

The parents take the child to the four quarters, saying:

> *Spirit of the [direction], behold [child's name]*
> *Welcome her to this world.*

They then pass her among those present. Each kisses her and says:

> *Welcome, [child's name]:*
> *Much love to you.*

It is also traditional for each person present to give a blessing or expression of best wishes. When the child reaches the guardians, they say:

> *Welcome, [child's name]:*
> *May you love as you will always be loved.*

The parents say the same when the child is returned to them. At the end of the ritual, the priestess says farewell to the gods:

> *Holy Ones, we thank you*
> *For the gift of life*
> *and the beauty of the world in which to live it*

> *For the gift of love*
> *and the wonderful people with which to share it.*
> *But most of all today for [child's name],*
> *who is both life and love.*
> *We ask your blessings as you depart.*
> *Hail and farewell.*

The priestess then dismisses the spirits of the directions, saying:

> *Spirit of the [direction],*
> *We thank you for your help.*
> *Go now in peace, but be never far away*
> *and answer quickly when [child's name] calls for you*
> *that you might aid her in her need.*

If you practice in the Celtic or Germanic traditions, you'll be setting up and presenting the child to the well, fire, and tree instead of the elements and directions. When you set up the well, say:

> *We establish the Well in our midst.*
> *May it provide life and inspiration to the child we bring*
>   *before it,*
> *today, and throughout her life.*

When you set up the tree, say:

> *We establish the Tree in our midst*
> *May it provide life and power to the child we bring before it,*
> *today, and throughout her life.*

When you set up the fire, say:

> *We establish this Fire in our midst.*
> *May it provide life and the presence of the sacred to the child*
>   *we bring before it,*
> *today, and throughout her life.*

Instead of blessing the child by the elements, present her to the well, saying:

> *Little one, receive the blessing of the Well,*
> *source of life,*
> *source of inspiration.*
> *May you be blessed with both as you go about your life.*

Present her to the tree, saying:

> *Little one, receive the blessing of the Tree,*
> *supporter of the Cosmos,*
> *form of all that is.*
> *May you be blessed with both as you go about your life.*

Present her to the fire, saying:

> *Little one, receive the blessing of the Fire,*
> *through which we make our offerings,*
> *which connects us with the sacred.*
> *May it serve both purposes for you.*
> *May you be blessed with both as you go about your life.*

Birthdays

In American culture, birthdays are already traditional ritual occasions. There's a song, food, candle-lighting, gift-giving, and wish-making—all earmarks of a folk festival. As Pagans, we shouldn't want to take anything away from this.

But more could be added. Most families, in fact, have their own special traditions. Some of these are passed on through the family, some have ethnic sources, and some are made up on the spot. Some you do once and discover the next year that your child considers them tradition.

When children get up on the morning of their birthday, have them wash and dress in special clothes, which may have been given the night before as an early birthday present. Then take them to the family shrine, light the hearth fire, and then light the shrine fire from it. Children who are old enough can light the fire themselves; a parent can do it for those who are too young. Once the fires are lit, the child makes an offering, which can be of incense, food, drink, or flowers. There should always be something offered; it's only right to give something in return for the great gift of a year. This offering should be accompanied by a short prayer. Here are some examples:

Birthday Prayer of Thanks

The wheel has turned again since I came into this world.
I thank the Holy Ones.
I thank the Ancestors.
I thank the Guardians of my house.
I thank the Spirits of the Land.
Thank you for everything you have done for me in this year.
Be with me in my new year
and I will remember you.

Birthday Prayer to the Ancestors

Ancestors
Old Ones
You who have lived before me:
I am here to show you that I have not forgotten you.
Thank you for helping me to grow through the year.
Help me to grow through the year to come.

Birthday Prayer to the Mother and Father

Mother of Everything
Father of Everything
Thank you for everything.
Here are some gifts for you
for all you have done.

Children who are old enough can compose their own prayers. The prayers don't have to be the same each year. Indeed, it's good for them to reflect the child's growing knowledge of the sacred. After the prayer and offering, extinguish the shrine fire and then the hearth fire. After the birthday, take whatever offerings are left out to your yard or to a wild place and leave them there.

Feasting with the Guardians

One of the meals on a child's birthday should be eaten with just the family present. Put the household guardian images on the table, along with the image of the child's personal guardian from the family shrine if the child has one. Make sure that this personal guardian receives some of each kind of food. At the end of the meal, the parents say:

> *The year has turned [age of child] times since you were born*
> *and now it has turned again.*
> *The gods have watched you grow*
> *and will stay with you as this next year turns.*

Then each parent blesses the child with a personal blessing written for the occasion. An example of a short one would be:

> *May the Lord and Lady bless you*
> *and watch and guard you*
> *as you grow through the year to come.*

Follow this with a party. This is the time for the family to give presents. Oh, and give the kid the day off from school. It is, after all, their day, and it only comes once a year.

CHAPTER 5

Teaching Children

Many of the character traits pagans want their children to have when they grow up aren't uniquely Pagan. We want our children to be honest, responsible, helpful, intelligent, loving, hospitable, honorable, and happy. Who doesn't? These are the common values of our culture.

Paganism's major contribution to values is its attitude toward nature. Helpful, yes, but not just to humans. Intelligent, yes, but not at the expense of the planet. Much of Pagan child-rearing, then, is geared toward developing a love of the world. Less emphasis is placed on things that seem specifically religious—beliefs, for instance—and more on living good lives. The usual religious things are important too, and our children must be taught them, but without the right attitude toward the world, they are useless and perhaps even harmful.

Pagan child-rearing isn't a one-shot thing: "This is what we believe and do; now run along." Nor is it even a set course: "Fulfill these lesson requirements and you'll be all set." At its best, teaching Pagan children goes on all the time. You compost, you turn off lights when you're not using them, you work in the garden, you perform the rituals. And you make sure your child is doing these things along with you. Remember: Paganism is a religion of *doing*. Much of your teaching will take place when you're performing rituals like those in this book.

Children learn best by parental example, second best by discovering through doing, and third best by active teaching. The more fully you live a Pagan life, the more your child will learn about Paganism, and the more they'll want to live a Pagan life as well. Teaching through doing involves many different types of activities and practices, and the rituals given here are important teaching tools, because they show what a Pagan *does*. Many other activities provide useful teaching as well. At the very least, you'll have to explain why you do the things you do. Children are very good at asking why.

Teaching by Doing

When choosing activities for young children, it's important to remember that you're not training priests or priestesses. You're working with children, trying to awaken them spiritually and give them a framework in which to do it. Here are some activities for your children to do to learn to walk the Pagan path.

Meditation

There are many forms of meditation, from the quiet contentless sitting of zazen to the more active forms involving chanting or dance. The very quiet forms can be hard for young children. Still, it's good training for them; it might help them learn how to sit still and focus their attention for a while. The concentration they learn from it will help them in other areas like schoolwork or when they start doing rituals on their own.

Try starting with short times: two minutes, for instance. If your child reacts poorly, back off for a while. Let them see you do it, and make sure they know that they can meditate too when they're old enough. The magic words "You can do this when you're old enough" are a great motivator for children. Don't be discouraged if your children are uncooperative at first. My daughter hated meditating, so we stopped. Then I discovered, some time later, that she'd been meditating on her own. Plant the seed, and let it grow.

To introduce children to meditation, have them sit with their back straight, their body relaxed, and their hands in their lap. You can have them try to sit in the lotus position, with their legs crossed one over the other. Children are very flexible and very proud of their ability to sit in unusual positions. This is especially true if you have trouble doing that yourself. Have them sit with a pillow under their rump so their knees can both touch the ground. This will also help them keep their backs straight. Alternatively, you can ask them to kneel and sit back on their heels. Or they can even just sit in a chair. Have them breathe slowly and evenly, being sure to push from the diaphragm rather than breathing more shallowly from the chest, counting their breaths either on the inhale, the exhale, or both. Have them count to five and then start over.

Self-blessings

Self-blessings are short rituals that children can do on their own. Here's a very simple one that can be done with a bowl of water or olive or corn oil. The child holds their hands over the bowl and says:

> *May this water [or oil] be blessed with the power of the gods*
> *so it will bless me.*

Then the child anoints themself with the oil or water. The places of the body that are blessed can vary, but usually the forehead is included. If they are preparing for work or sports, they may wish to anoint the parts of their bodies used in those activities. Self-blessings can also be used as part of morning or evening prayers.

Masks

Masks have long been used by Pagans—to change shamans into their power animals, to invoke gods and ancestors into their worshippers, and to transform actors in sacred drama into the deities they represent. Masks therefore straddle the border between fantasy and reality, as well as that between magic and fun. They can give power, teach a child to identify with an animal or spirit, free a child from normal constraints, and just be fun. With a mask, a child can be something different, trying on new ways of being for size.

In chapter 3, I talked about using masks as guardian images, but their uses can go far beyond that. And making masks is a great activity for children. The easiest material to make masks from is paper. Temporary masks can be made from paper bags or cardboard. A paper plate, for example, can be turned into a mask by cutting eye and mouth holes and punching a hole on each side for strings or elastic to hold it on. Faces and designs can then be drawn on them with crayons, markers, or paint. Small feathers, ribbons, and seeds can be glued on to decorate them. Other items such as large feathers can be attached with ribbon. More permanent masks can be made with papier-mâché (see chapter 3).

God's Eyes

"God's Eyes" are designs made from two sticks and colored yarn. Made in elemental colors or dedicated to different gods, they can be used to mark the edges of sacred space. They can also sit in the family shrine as symbols of the household guardians. Made large in the color of a particular spiritual being, with smaller crosslets at the ends of the sticks in the elemental colors, they can also be used to create a protective wall hanging. Yellow ones make good solar decorations; white ones can be used to represent the moon.

To make a God's Eye, take two or more sticks or dowels and cross them in the middle. Tie the sticks together with the end of a long piece of yarn. Wrap the yarn around one stick, looping it over. Then wrap the yarn around the next stick, this time looping it under. Keep doing this, alternating the direction of looping, until you run out of yarn or sticks, or until the God's Eye is big enough for your purposes. Leave some of the sticks protruding from the yarn when you're done to prevent the last loop from slipping off. Tie the last bit off and cut the yarn flush with the knot. Colors can be changed as you move outward, either mixing different colors or using two or more shades of one color.

Personal Shrines

Children can make personal shrines in their own rooms. This kind of shrine should have a deity figure as a focus and be used for devotion rather than magical work. Teach your children some simple self-blessings and worship rituals, and then leave them to it. Tell them to perform some ritual at the shrine at least once a day, at a regular time—first thing in the morning, last thing at night, or both—for a month. Don't interfere, though. The best way to ensure they perform these kinds of prayers is to allow them to see that you're doing them too.

How complicated the shrine is will depend on the age of the child. Younger children may be content with a statue or drawing, a bowl for offerings, and a bowl of water for purification. Older children can use candles and incense once they've been taught how to handle them safely. The kind of rituals performed at these shrines will also vary. For young children, you'll most likely need to write a short prayer or two that they can use. Older children can write their own prayers or wait for the deity to inspire one in them.

At one point in her training, I had my daughter look through books on deities and choose one to have a shrine to. She chose the Shinto goddess Amaterasu, whose main symbol is a mirror, so I bought a small one to use for her in the shrine. I wrote a small ritual, taught her how to do it, and then had her perform it first thing in the morning for a month. I deliberately told her only the minimum about the goddess, in order to see what would happen. At the end of the month, I asked her how the rituals had gone, and she asked me if Amaterasu was connected with the sea. She is indeed, but that was something I hadn't told my daughter. This is a good example of how exercises like this can lead a child to a personal experience of deity.

Rattles

Rattles can be made from many things. The most traditional of them is gourds. Choose one with no blemishes. Some gourds can simply be dried, leaving the seeds inside to make the sounds. Usually, though, they need help. Cut off the gourd's end and scrape out as much of the flesh as you can. Keep the gourd in a warm, dry place until it's completely dry. If you leave too much flesh behind or if the gourd isn't dried carefully, it can become moldy. When it's dry, put some of the seeds back in, along with some pebbles, and plug up the end.

Making a rattle out of papier-mâché can be easier, especially when working with children. Blow up a balloon to the desired size and cover it with strips of paper soaked in wallpaper paste. Put on several layers for strength, alternating the direction in which you lay the strips. Leave a thin spot at the top and an open spot at the bottom for the stick. When the rattle is dry, remove the balloon. (It will probably have collapsed already; if not, just pop it.)

After removing the balloon, put noisemakers inside. It's traditional to include both quartz pebbles and seeds; popcorn works fine for seeds. Shape a stick or dowel to fit the hole in the bottom, or fit the hole to the size of the stick. Carve the top of the stick so that it's thinner than the rest. After filling the rattle with the noisemakers, put the stick through the bottom hole. Where it touches the top of the rattle, make a hole just large enough for it to pass through. Seal the two holes, top and bottom, with more strips of paper and extra glue. When the glue is completely dry, decorate the rattle with paint, feathers, or ribbons.

Easier still is to make a rattle from a small plastic bottle, like an empty vitamin bottle, partly filled with pebbles and seeds. Put the top back on, and you have an instant rattle. You can glue paper around it and let children draw whatever they want on it.

Images

Children can make images for their personal shrines or make them for the household shrine. They can use clay or papier-mâché to make statues, or they can draw or paint images on paper, cardboard, or wood. Collages made of seeds, sticks, or stones are also fun to make and can work well as images.

Nature Journals

Help your child keep track of the seasons for one year, noting the dates that plants flower, the times when leaves appear or change color or fall, the migrations of birds, the behavior of animals, weather patterns, etc.

Observe a Space

Choose an area about one yard square and mark it off. On your own land, you can do this with rope. On public land, you can use natural features to define the space or mark it with sticks pushed flush into the ground. With your child, observe the space for one hour a day over a short period of time (two weeks, for instance). Then observe it weekly for a longer period of time (several months to a year). Call on the spirits of the place each time you and your child observe. Don't interfere with the space; just observe it. Help your child keep track of the changes.

Gardening

Have your child choose the plants for a garden, then plant them, care for them, harvest them, and prepare the garden for winter. The size and complexity of the garden can vary with the age of the child. Have your child write and carry out a garden blessing. Remember that a garden can be planted in a window box, or in pots on a balcony, or even indoors—for instance, an herb garden kept by a sunny window.

Costume Parties

Invite your children's friends to come to a party dressed as mythical characters. You may have to limit this to Pagan children.

Chanting, Singing, and Drumming

Children love to sing, and so do Pagans. See the resources section at the back of the book for a list of some recordings of Pagan songs.

Drumming is the best thing that ever happened to Neo-Paganism, and the earlier a child gets involved in it the better. Drums can be used for communication, for dance rhythms to accompany songs, or for just plain fun. Drum with your child yourself, either with just your own drums or keeping a beat to recorded music. You can use rattles instead of drums, or along with them. Once a child can keep a simple beat, encourage them to bring their drums to a Pagan gathering. There will probably be rituals they can participate in. The experience of being part of a group of drummers contributing to a ritual is overpowering. Children have few opportunities to take part in rituals in such an active way.

Inexpensive drums are available in music and toy stores. I've bought quite a few at Disney World. You can order small, good-quality frame drums online. For an even less expensive drum, you can use a shoebox, an oatmeal box, or a plastic container.

Storytelling

Stories can be myths, fairy tales, or just fictions made up on the spot. They can be told by parents to children, or by children to parents. They can be related "round-robin," with someone starting a story and then handing it off to someone else, who then has to continue the tale for a while before passing it on again. Hearing and telling the old stories is one of the most important things that can happen in a Pagan child's life. The stories are a link with the Pagans of old times, and they also serve as models for ritual and life.

When telling stories, use all your abilities. Use props and different voices, and don't be afraid to embroider the tales, provided you preserve their essential elements.

Decorations

Children love to make decorations for celebrations. One easy way to make them is to roll polymer clay to between ⅛" and ¼" thick and then use cookie cutters or table knives to cut suitable shapes—moons, suns, or seasonal symbols, for instance. Bake the shapes according to the directions on the package. (Different types and thicknesses may require different times and temperatures.) Decorate them by scratching designs into them before baking them, or paint them after they're baked.

Guided Meditation

Guided meditations bridge the gap between the instruction required by a beginner and the imagination desired in the more advanced practitioner. They do this by providing a descriptive frame for a journey or image, while leaving details to the meditator. This allows children to be guided, yet encourages them to contribute to the meditation.

Many books and recordings give texts for guided meditation. Here I've given one for an encounter with the Wiccan Goddess that puts an emphasis on a child forming their own image, and one for encountering the Wiccan God in which the image is more defined.

Guided meditations are commonly used for encountering a deity. You can write your own with a little research. After choosing a deity, read the relevant myths and seek out photographs or drawings of images to determine the deity's appearance, as well as the types of scenes in which that deity might be found and the teachings they might impart.

As with all meditation, the goal is to be both relaxed and alert. Start with whatever meditation work you usually do with your child. Then read the text below in a slow, soft voice. You can accompany the words with quiet drumming, increasing the rhythm as you go to increase the meditation's impact. When the meditation's over, it's best for the child to remain for a while in the same position, breathing slowly, before returning to normal awareness.

Guided Meditation for the Goddess

The goal of this meditation is to encourage children to form an image of the Goddess that will help them imagine her more clearly. It can be done as a preparation for making a physical image of the Goddess or simply to help a child in their devotions. In the course of the meditation, the Goddess gives a teaching that will be unique each time it is done.

Have the child sit in their usual meditation position. Read the text slowly, pausing to give them time to think when it's called for.

> *We are going to imagine the Great Mother.*
> *It is good to imagine.*
> *Imagination is halfway to magic.*
> *If you keep imagining the Goddess you will find she*
> *   becomes real*
> *and then your imagining will have become real.*
> *You will have built her a road to come to you on.*
> *She is everything, of course: Maiden, Mother, Crone.*
> *Today we are going to imagine the Mother.*
> *Think of her.*
> *She is strong.*
> *She is beautiful.*
> *She is peaceful.*
> *Ask yourself questions and put the answers in the image.*

Give the child time here to imagine an image of the Mother. Then continue, pausing after each question:

> *Is she sitting or standing?*
> *Is her skin dark or light?*
> *What is she wearing?*
> *Does she have jewelry?*
> *What color is her hair?*
> *How long is it?*
> *Is it curly or wavy or straight?*
> *How is it worn?*

What color is her skin?
What color are her eyes?
Is her nose small or large?
Wide or narrow?
Are her lips large or thin?
Are they dark or light?
Are her breasts large or small?
Are her hips narrow or wide?
How does she hold her hands?
Does she hold anything in them?

Give the child time again to fill in the details of the image. Then continue, pausing to give time to answer:

She says something to you.
What is it she says?
If you can't hear her, that's okay.
You can feel something, even if it isn't in words.

Let the child imagine the message the Mother may be giving. Then continue slowly, letting each statement sink in and become a part of the child's image:

She loves you.
She has the strength to help you.
It is yours when you want it.
When you are afraid
or worried
or just need a hug
and no one is around to help you
imagine her
and she will hold you in her arms.
Hold her image for a few more seconds
and then thank her and say goodbye.
Then let the image fade away.
But don't worry.

She is still with you.
She is everywhere.
Always.

Guided Meditation for the God

This is a different type of guided meditation. Here the child is given very specific imagery and a particular message. The point of this type of meditation is to convey what sort of imagery and teaching is associated with a particular deity. Before using this kind of meditation with a child, you have to be very sure of these yourself.

Begin speaking slowly and in a soft tone, encouraging the child to become immersed in the experience you're describing:

> *Imagine that you are in the woods. The trees around you are*
> *pines. There is just enough light to see by, but it comes to*
> *you from above the branches of the trees. The trees are*
> *very tall, and their branches don't start until very high*
> *up, higher than a house. Everything around you smells*
> *like pine. The ground is covered with needles. The trunks*
> *of the trees rise from these needles, straight and tall and*
> *rough and hard.*
> *You can hear birds in the branches, but you can't see them.*
> *Except for the birds, there is no noise at all. Sit for a sec-*
> *ond and imagine the trees and the birds and the quiet.*

Pause here to allow the child to enter into the space you've created. After a few moments, return to your description:

> *From somewhere in front of you, you start to hear a sound. It*
> *is the sound of a drum beating. It beats in time with your*
> *breathing. As you pay attention to it, it starts to sound*
> *louder, and now you can tell that it comes from directly*
> *in front of you.*

Walk toward the sound. As you walk, you find the way is
easy. There seems to be a path between the trees. May-
be deer have made it. The path leads just the way you
are going.
The pine needles on the ground are soft, like a carpet, so you
take your shoes and socks off and walk in your bare feet.
You keep walking through the woods. The trees are still
pines, but they start to grow closer together. You keep
walking, and soon they are so close together that you can't
fit between them anymore.
It's as if they have grown together into a wall. So you start
to follow the wall to your left. It starts to curve, and you
realize that it makes a circle. You look closely at the wall
as you walk, and you notice that, in some places, it's not so
solid. In fact, you find a place where, if you try really hard,
you might just be able to squeeze through. It looks hard,
but you are brave, so you push yourself through.

Again, pause to let the child enter fully into the scene you're describing
and absorb all the details you've given. After a moment or two, return
to the meditation:

On the other side of the wall is a clearing. It's still a little
dark, but, if you look straight up, you can see the sky.
And in the middle of the sky is a single star.
In the center of the clearing is a small hill. In the side of the
hill is a small cave. You go to the mouth of the cave and
look inside. There's a man sitting there looking back at
you. He's sitting cross-legged on the ground. He has antlers
growing from his head. His hair is rough and shaggy. He's
wearing pants that seem to be made of leather, but his
chest and feet are bare.
Now you notice that the man's smiling. On his lap is a bag
of coins. He takes one out and gives it to you. On one side
of it is a picture of the man. On the other side is the name

> *[use whatever name you usually use for the God here]. Of*
> *course, he isn't a man; he's a god. In fact, he is the God,*
> *the one who is the Father of Everything.*
> *The man says: "Keep this coin and, when you want to feel me*
> *near you, just imagine you are holding it in your hand."*
> *You thank him, and then he starts to fade away. Around*
> *you, the cave is also fading away, and the wall of trees,*
> *and the woods. You find yourself right back in your own*
> *home, back where you started. You open your eyes, and*
> *here you are.*
> *But in your pocket, you can feel the coin.*

Follow a guided meditation by talking with the child about it. If the meditation was a guided journey where contact with a deity or other spiritual being was made, you'll want to talk to the child about that deity.

Other Activities and Resources

There are many other activities and resources that can be useful when teaching children the Pagan way. Some that are sponsored by non-Pagans can still be part of a Pagan education. Summer camps and nature and science centers all teach knowledge of and respect for nature. Art museums sometimes give workshops in skills like mask-making. Community centers and ethnic societies give lessons in traditional dance and music. Watching certain videos can also be educational. Many movies play with mythical themes—*Star Wars*, *The NeverEnding Story*, *Camelot*, etc. Many Disney movies also involve mythical themes.

Don't forget extracurricular activities. Trips to museums, nature centers, the beach, or the woods—or even just a walk —can be very educational, especially if you don't point that out to your child. Other activities can include recycling, composting, or taking care of an animal. Older children should be given practical, living-in-the-world assignments to teach them how to live out their Paganism.

You can also choose about a dozen gods and goddesses and teach children about them one at a time over the course of several months. Describe their functions and explain how they can be called upon. Give their attributes and appearance to help children visualize them better. Make pictures of them with the child. If possible, teach about each of them at an appropriate place—Manannán at the seashore, Demeter in a garden, Thor under an oak tree.

Or you can choose a single deity for a child to work with. One way to do this is by taking about two dozen craft sticks (you can buy these at craft stores; they're essentially popsicle sticks) and writing the name of a deity on each one. Then have the child throw the sticks on the ground. Put aside the ones that land face down, and have the child cast the remaining sticks. Do this until only one stick remains face up. Put an image of that deity in a shrine for the child to pray to or practice rituals in honor of. When my daughter did this, the goddess chosen was Rhiannon, who was already her patron deity. Very impressive, and I think it had a strong impact on her.

CHAPTER 6

Pagan Prayers and Offerings

Prayer is a loaded word. Our childhood memories of prayer are sometimes unpleasant. And even our pleasant ones can cause problems for Pagans if they bring up Judeo-Christian associations. But remember two things. First, prayer is a perfectly Pagan thing to do. Many of our surviving records of ancient Paganism, from hieroglyphs on pyramid walls to cuneiform tablets, are of prayers. Don't let reactions to your childhood limit your religious practices. And second, your children don't have any childhood memories yet. It's up to you to make sure the ones they develop are good ones. Don't limit *their* religion in reaction to *your* childhood.

By understanding some of the objections raised to prayer, perhaps we can redeem the practice, not only for our children's sake, but for our own as well. For instance, prayer is often criticized as a rote activity. We all probably remember praying almost mindlessly, without paying attention to the meaning of the words. But what's wrong with that? Isn't that what we do when we chant? Is it really so much better to consciously dwell on the meaning of every word? Even a superficial glance at techniques used by the world's religions, including Pagan ones, turns up a variety of rote techniques—mantras and rosaries, for instance. The lack of conscious effort allowed by memorized prayers can shut our minds up long enough to allow the sacred to enter. Further, rote prayers are uniquely consoling in tragic circumstances. When something terrible happens, it's a great comfort not to have to think of words to express our emotions. A well-worn prayer comes to our lips, and we start to feel better.

Another common objection is to petitionary prayer. "Our relationship with the gods shouldn't include the word 'gimme.'" Or "They turn the sacred into a cosmic Santa Claus." Well, this may be true. But you grew out of it; trust that your children will too.

The old Pagan concept of petition was expressed in the Roman concept *do ut des*: "I give that you might give." Pagans therefore don't say "gimme." They say: "Here I am, doing what's right for me to do. Now you do what's right for *you* to do." And after their prayers are fulfilled, they thank the gods. So Pagan petitionary prayer teaches personal responsibility and gratitude, not cosmic materialism.

Petitionary prayer can be a wonderful thing for a child. Children often feel helpless when loved ones are suffering. They're often too young to help by either material or magical means. But if they can pray, then they can help. Their prayers can also reinforce caring for others, if they don't pray only for themselves

But not all prayers ask for something. Prayers of praise and presence are an introduction to what may later become mysticism. Prayers to sacred spots, trees, rocks, animals, and other natural features teach respect for the world; they say, "The world does not belong to humans alone." So all in all, prayer is not only beneficial; it's a very Pagan thing to do. The ancient Pagans did it; they must have been on to something.

Prayers for Children

Prayers for children are best kept short and poetic. If they rhyme or have a strong meter they're easier for children to memorize. And while prayers that have a sing-song effect may repel an adult, they're often loved by children.

Here are some sample prayers.

Prayer to Establish Sacred Space

Here in the center of the world I stand,
Earth is before me,
Air on my right hand,
Fire is behind me,
on my left Water lies,
as I stand here between
the earth and the skies.

Prayers to the Gods and Goddesses

Mother of All
Queen of the Earth
Here I am,
One of your children.
Help me to be the best I can be
so that people will know
the wonder of you.

♦ ♦ ♦

She's with me
and hugs me
and loves me
and keeps me
as safe as can be
my Goddess, my Mother.
I'm with her
and hug her
and love her
and keep her
inside in my heart
my Goddess, my Mother.

♦ ♦ ♦

Thank you, dear Mother, for giving us birth.
Thank you, dear Goddess, the Great Mother Earth.
The bright moon above me shines her soft light
and kisses me standing here hugged by the night.

♦ ♦ ♦

Thor, my helper and great protector,
watch over and guard me by night and by day.

♦ ♦ ♦

Freyja, come to me,
your cart pulled by cats,
and give me the gifts
I know you provide.

♦ ♦ ♦

Brigid, who protects
our heart and our home,
protect me as well,
whether there or without.

♦ ♦ ♦

Isis, extend your wings over me,
protecting me daily,
and when I'm asleep.

Morning Prayers

Good morning, world, and good morning, sun.
I greet the new day with my arms spread wide
and thank the gods for the dreams they sent.

♦ ♦ ♦

It's daytime again,
and time to get up.
Look down on me, Sun,
as I go through my day.
Help me to learn
and be good
and be kind
to all of the people
I meet on my way.

Mealtime Prayers

Eating is a sacred act. By eating, we take part in the mysteries of life
and death. It's especially incumbent on meat-eaters to remember those
who've died to make their food, but even vegetarians take lives in order
to live. That's the way it is, and the life of a lentil is as sacred as the life
of a lamb.

Praying before meals is thus always appropriate, although you may
want to have a short version for everyday use and a longer one for special
occasions such as festivals, moon observances, or weekly family-night
meals. Here are some simple mealtime prayers:

We thank the spirits of the land who gave us this food.
We thank the women and men who grew it and prepared it.
We thank all the gods and all of the goddesses.
We bless this food in their names.

♦ ♦ ♦

Food is the gift of the Earth,
Warmed and lit by the Sun
Coming from the Goddess
by the power of the God.
We are blessed by eating it.

♦ ♦ ♦

We thank the plants and animals
whose deaths make our lives.
We thank all the gods
Who bring death and life.

♦ ♦ ♦

Isn't it wonderful?
Look at this food.
Where did it come from?
How did it get here?
The Earth gave birth to it.
The Sun fed it.
The waters filled it.
People cared for it.
And when it was time,
it was harvested for us.
People prepared it and now it is here for us.
Thank you, Earth.
Thank you, Sun.
Thank you, waters.
Thank you, people.
It is indeed wonderful.

♦ ♦ ♦

Blessings to the Spirits of the Land.
Blessings to the Guardians of our family.
Blessings to all the gods and goddesses.
Blessings upon the food we will eat tonight.

For special occasions, a more complex grace might be desired. Before the meal, prepare as much of the food as possible as a family. Set the table with special dishes, linens, and candles. Establish sacred time and light the candles, saying:

In the light of these flames there is peace.
May all on whom they shine be blessed.
May those blessings extend through all the world
and fall on all who dwell in it.

Follow this with a short prayer, such as one of those above, said by someone else to create a break between the two prayers. Put a small portion of each food on a plate to be put in the family shrine later as an offering. Alternatively, ask one of the children to bring the plate to the shrine at this time. As you place the food on the plate, say:

We share our fortune with our household guardians.

At the end of the meal, blow out the candles and end sacred time in your usual way. Then everybody should help clean up.

Bedtime Prayers

Prayers at the end of the day create a bookend with ones in the morning, making the entire day sacred. They also lead into a time of dreams, when sacred beings may be encountered, problems solved, or important truths conveyed.

The Great Horned Lord, the bringer of dreams,
rides through the night on roads of moonbeams.
Please give me your gifts of visions and sight
as I lie in my bed, asleep in the night.

◆　◆　◆

Lord of Dreams
I pray to you at the end of the day.
Lady of Sleep
I pray to you at the start of the night.
Send me sleep and send me dreams
restful and sweet till I wake up again.

♦ ♦ ♦

Mother of Everything, wrap me in your arms,
and carry me off to the land of dreams.

♦ ♦ ♦

As I go to sleep I think of all the others with whom I
*   share this world*
and I ask all the Holy Ones:
the gods and the goddesses, the spirits, the ancestors,
all who watch over my family,
to bless them all and make them happy.

♦ ♦ ♦

Blessed be the goddesses.
Blessed be the gods.
Blessed be all their children everywhere.

♦ ♦ ♦

Lug, whose spear protects the world,
whose teaching gives help to grow our food:
may all who sleep be watched over well,
and all of our dreams be lovely.

♦ ♦ ♦

Hypnos, who brings good sleep and good dreams,
provide them this night as I pray to you.

Bedtime is also a good time to bless a child. This can be particularly helpful if the child has been having nightmares. Trace a protective symbol (see Appendix A) on the child's forehead with water or olive or corn oil while saying something like:

May the Holy Ones bless you
and your dreams be pleasant.

Prayers for a Child Leaving Home

When a child leaves the home, whether to move out or just for a long trip, they should be blessed by the parents. This extends the protection of the gods and the household guardians over them while they're away. These blessings may include the name of a deity of travelers such as Woden or Hermes, or one who's a protector, like Isis or Lug.

A child who's moving out of the parental home will need to tell the guardians of this, and leave them an offering. The person giving the blessing holds their hands over the head of the child while reciting the prayer. These should be suited to the child and the occasion. Here are some examples:

May She bless you while you are far from home
May He guide you on your way
May you return in safety to your home
to those who love you and wait for you.

♦ ♦ ♦

The blessings of Woden upon this traveler.
May he make your path clear before you
and smooth out difficulties before they arise.

♦ ♦ ♦

Our Lady Isis wraps her wings around you:
Rest securely in them, and know you will be safe.

♦ ♦ ♦

You go on your way to see many new things.
Do not waste this chance to learn of the world.
Keep your eyes open
Keep your ears ready
And return better than you left.
You go under the protection of the gods
and the hands of the guardians will be with you
*   wherever you go.*

♦ ♦ ♦

I bless you with the blessing of our Lady.
I bless you with the blessing of our Lord.
I send you on your way marked with their sign
that all who meet you might know of their power.
Remember, you are their child:
Do nothing to shame them.
They will not forsake you.

♦ ♦ ♦

I call upon the guardians of our family
to keep their protection over this child who will be away
    from our home.
He/She may go far from the shrine of the guardians,
but they will continue to watch over him/her.

♦ ♦ ♦

No matter where you travel, it will be on the Earth.
No matter where you travel it will be under the Sky.
They will watch over you
They will care for you
They will not forget you
They will love you with a parent's love
as we love you with a parent's love.
Our blessing goes with you.

♦ ♦ ♦

You are going into the place of another people,
a place with its own guardians, its own spirits, its own gods
    and goddesses.
Yours will go with you.
Greet theirs with respect and reverence.
May they be your friends even as those of this place are.

Offerings

The giving of offerings to deities, spirits, and ancestors is an ancient practice that may well be the most common religious act in the world. Many of the treasures we have from ancient cultures are offerings that were buried or thrown into water. The Battersea shield, the statues from the source of the Seine: what wonderful devotion was expressed in giving these masterpieces to the gods. And how many more humble offerings of food and drink must have been made!

Like prayers, an offering can sometimes be in the nature of a business deal—I give you this, O god; now give me that. Maybe it doesn't seem the most mature relationship to have with the sacred, but it has many years of tradition to back it up. Indeed, it's a right and just thing to do. The gods appreciate justice and will acknowledge fair dealings. Remember the principle of *do ut des*.

An offering may mean other things, though. It can be a way of saying to a deity: "See, you're important to me, important enough that I'm willing to give these things up for you." It can be an expression of gratitude, an acknowledgment of indebtedness: "I know that what I got, I got with your help, so this is your share." There are many altars set up by Romans that have inscriptions on them that tell us that they were set up in fulfillment of a vow. And, like all exchanges, offerings can help establish or solidify a relationship: "We give each other things; that's what friends do."

Offerings can be many different things. They can be libations poured on the ground, food, incense, or even hair. In fact, hair is often given as a gift to ancestors; we recognize that our bodies come from them, so we give some of that body back. Hair is especially suitable to offer at rites of passage; we give up a part of ourselves as a sign that our old selves are passing away. The cutting of hair is also a traditional sign of mourning to show that, with the death of a loved one, we have lost a piece of ourselves.

The offerings suggested for different kinds of spirits and deities in Appendix B are drawn from many cultures. The list reveals patterns: certain types of spirits prefer certain types of gifts. Location plays a part as well. For instance, American nature spirits are fond of cornmeal and tobacco, both from plants native to this country. All grains are considered good, as are prepared food and drink, artwork, songs, and our time and labor. In fact, anything that's of value to us is worthy of being used as an offering—but more important, anything that's of value to the deity it's offered to.

If you want to make offerings to a specific deity but don't know what they favor, there are three courses open to you. First, you can offer what my daughter calls "the usual"—grain (preferably cooked by you, so as to add your own gift), and beer or wine. Second, you can do some research. The resources given at the back of the book are some places for this. The best place to start is probably *Funk & Wagnalls Standard Dictionary of Folklore, Mythology, and Legend.* Then move on to sources that deal with the appropriate culture. Third, you can simply ask the deities or spirits concerned what they like. Follow the same steps you would for making an offering, but when you reach the part where the actual offering would be given, instead ask the deity what they prefer. Listen carefully, with your intuition as well as your ears, and if you receive an answer, thank the deity and go get the requested item. Then return and start the offering again.

The general procedure for making offerings is simple. First, stand or sit for a few moments, dwelling on the sacredness of the spot. Remember, all places are sacred, although some may appear to be more sacred than others—an ancient tree, a weathered stone, the border between your yard and your neighbor's, your stove as it cooks your food. But in fact, what we perceive as a lack of sacredness in some places is really a lack of sacredness in ourselves, not in those places. We're simply blind to their holiness.

The way to overcome this blindness is to open your eyes, to *really* open your eyes. What you see is usually as dependent on what you *expect* to see as it is on what's actually there. To see the sacred in every spot, you have to stop your expectations and judgments and let the spot be what it is.

First pay attention to the place, without making any judgments, not even naming what happens. For instance, suppose a wasp flies by. Don't think: "Wasp; I'm afraid of them." Don't think: "Wasp; important for pest control." Don't even think: "Wasp." Just let the wasp fly by, being what it is. This is a way to honor the place by allowing everything in it to be what it is, without interference.

After you have honored the place, establish sacred time and call the spirit you're going to offer to. You can do this out loud, calling the spirit's name or title. But many spirits, especially nature spirits, have no names, at least none they will tell us. For these, you can follow the Roman practice and call out to "the spirit of this place, whether god or goddess." You can also do this silently, concentrating on finding a mental picture of the spirit.

Once you can feel the presence of the spirit, make your offering. If you don't feel them, make the offering anyway. Sometimes the very act of giving an offering will bring a spirit to you. Offerings seem to open a conduit between our world and that of sacred beings. Or, as I like to say: "Presents create presence."

Whatever words you're using can be said before, during, or after the offering is placed. (I prefer to speak during the offering, because that identifies the words and the action; neither is given more value, so the physical object offered and the action performed with it aren't different from the nonmaterial offering—the words spoken—in any significant way.) What you say will vary with your intent, the spirit to whom the offering is made, and your relationship with that spirit.

Offering Prayer for Children

When you teach your children to make offerings, explain why they are making them. Help them to make offerings whenever possible and appropriate, and make sure there are suitable items available to them so they can make offerings on their own. Whenever a ritual calls for an offering, consider allowing the child to make it. Here is a typical offering prayer:

> *We give of ours.*
> *You give of yours.*

[Name or title of the spirit], here is a gift.
I am your friend.
Be my friend, too.

After the offering is placed, sit or stand a moment or two, again dwelling on the sacredness of the place, then thank the spirit for its attention and leave respectfully.

Indoor offerings can be made into bowls, used only for offerings and kept in your household shrine, or you can use your everyday bowls or your best china. Allow the offerings to stay for at least twenty-four hours and then take them outdoors. They can be taken into your yard, to a roadside, or to a river, lake, or harbor. Leftover liquid offerings can be given to Cloacina, if you've invited her into your home.

CHAPTER 7

The Cycle of the Moon

One reason Paganism has caught the imagination of so many is its recognition of the female side of divinity. Although, on the abstract theological level, the Judeo-Christian God most of us grew up with is beyond gender, in his everyday manifestations he has been seen as exclusively male. And now a religion comes along that claims that the divine is at least equally female. This concept has been transformative for many women—and not a few men.

Neo-Pagans revere a multitude of female deities. The one that's most worshipped by Wiccans is the Goddess, the Mother of All. She's just what her title says: the mother of all phenomena, living or not. She's a mother in all meanings of the word—the giver of birth, the nourisher, the teacher, and the one who disciplines. Many Neo-Pagans see the other goddesses worshipped throughout the world as simply her different faces. Others choose to see other goddesses as separate, but in some sense lesser, while still others don't even worship an overarching goddess. Wiccans, though, who form a majority of Neo-Pagans, worship the Goddess, in some form, whom they generally connect with the moon, as was often done in the Mediterranean region in antiquity, and this chapter will therefore be directed mostly by this idea.

Because of its attributes and identity, Wiccans give the moon special reverence. It shines down on everyone in the world, always changing yet always the same. Even when the moon can't be seen, its presence is felt. Even when it's apparently gone, the moon sends us blessings and teachings. As Queen of the Night, the moon is the guardian of secrets. Because of the connection between the menstrual cycle and the lunar cycle, the moon is seen as the patroness of women's mysteries. It rules the seas and our bodies in the tides. And its affect on lovers is well known.

As the moon moves through its phases, it shows us the different faces of the Goddess. When the moon is waxing, she's the Maiden, the young and developing woman, the dancer and singer. When the moon is full, she's the Mother, she who holds us safe in her arms and on whom we can call for help. And when the moon is dark, she's the Crone, the wise woman who teaches us her wisdom; she holds nothing back if we have the strength to learn from her, and it is she who will call us to her in the end.

The moon taught our ancestors to measure time. Day and night are a flickering of light and the year passes slowly, but the moon is our clock in the sky. In fact, the word "month" is related to "moon," as are the roots of words we use for measurement. The earliest measurements that have been yet discovered are scratches on bone and stone that may have recorded the moon's phases.

It's the Dark Moon and the Full Moon that are most commonly celebrated by Wiccans, as the opposing points of Mother and Crone, the cusps on which the changes occur. The return of the moon is also a fitting day for celebration, though. The Goddess hasn't died; she's been changed, and life goes on. Indeed, this is a monthly reminder that life continues, even after seeming death.

That's why some say it was the moon's cycle that inspired a belief in rebirth. It's certain that it holds deep mysteries of change without death, of growth, of womanhood. Knowledge of these comes with maturity and practice. These mysteries are taught in covens and in women's lodges; knowledge of them is granted to those who meditate on the moon.

In their fullness, the moon's mysteries aren't dealt with easily in a family context. But even very young children can follow the moon's phases. They can be taught the names of the phases, their shapes, and their times of rising. And you can add to this knowledge by encouraging a ritual awareness of the moon's cycles. The mysteries of the changing of the moon will come to children in time.

Children are taught by myth, example, ritual, and experience. Family moon rituals for very young children, though, shouldn't be heavy-handed; keep them simple and clear. It's enough at first to observe three of the moon's phases: the dark, the return, and the full. Time and the Goddess will do the rest.

Since the Bible forbids kissing one's hand to the moon (Job 31:26-7) it's a pretty good bet this was a Pagan custom. This can be done by forming the "horned hand," something that's easily taught to children. To do this, you make a fist with your dominant hand and extend your index and little fingers. Kiss that hand and then extend it toward the moon so you can see it cradled between the horns. Children can greet the moon this way each night when they see her for the first time, especially on her return.

CELEBRATING THE MOON

Decorations: Mirrors, crystals, white and silver ribbons. Or make a moon hanging by braiding three ribbons or cords together. Use white, silver, and light blue, or white, light blue, and dark blue, or white, red, and black. These last three are used by some Pagans to symbolize the three phases of the moon—Maiden, Mother, and Crone, respectively. Braid only part of the ribbons, then tie them off and leave the rest hanging. Attach the braided end to the back of a round mirror, a silver metal disk, or a wooden disk painted silver, and hang it on the wall, perhaps in the household shrine.

Making a Moon Candle

The moon rituals given here involve a moon candle. This is a large white or silver candle, preferably unscented, since different scents are often associated with different phases. Its base can be decorated by you or the children, and you can help them cut designs into the candle with a hot knife. Keep the candle in your household shrine as a companion to your sun candle (see chapter 8). In the rituals given here, the candle is put on the table for moon festivals.

Dark Moon

The Dark Moon a time of great mystery, when deep changes take place in the souls of women and men who are in tune with it. These are personal mysteries, private changes, and are thus especially appropriate for adolescents, who are undergoing their own mysterious changes. For younger children, though, don't play too heavily on the deep changes of the dark moon. Their time will come, all too soon.

The rituals below include strong symbols of the moon hidden away and an emphasis on dreams. These will plant a seed, to raise an awareness of the moon as a spiritual force, which is what we want most for our children when they are young.

For these rituals, use your best plates and serve some dark-moon foods. For drinks you can use something like iced tea or colas. For dessert, you can use hermit, oatmeal, or chocolate cookies, or gingerbread, or something else made with molasses or brown sugar. Put the moon candle in the center of the table. In front of one of the children's plates, put a square or circle of black or dark-blue cloth. (If you have more than one child, take turns.) Establish sacred time, but without lighting any candles, even the moon candle.

Dark Moon Ritual

At a sign from one of the adults, one of the children says:

> *Why is tonight special?*

An adult answers:

> *Tonight is the Dark Moon.*

The same child (or another one) says:

> *Why is this a special time?*

An adult answers:

> *The Dark Moon is the Alone Time,*
> *time to be by yourself in quiet,*
> *to dream of the changes you are going through*
> *and to honor the changes you have made*
> *since the last time the Moon was dark.*

(These questions were inspired by those asked and answered in Jewish celebrations of Passover.)

The questions can instead be asked by the adults and the answers given by the children. As they grow, their understanding of the day will change and this ritual will be a regular opportunity for them to express their increased knowledge. Allowing the child to take the usual adult role is one way to mark a coming of age.

The child who has the cloth in front of them picks it up, holds it over the moon candle, and then drops it, arranging it so that it completely covers the candle. The mother (or one of the adults) holds her hands over the covered candle and says:

> *The sky is dark with no Moon to be seen.*
> *She is hidden in secret to make Herself new.*
> *The Moon is dark tonight as She passes from light to light.*

Alternatively, after arranging things as described above, one of the adults can say:

> Shh.
> It is dark tonight, with no moon to light our way.
> Shh.

One of the adults says:

> The sky will be dark tonight, with no moon to light our way.
> She is hidden in the dark to make herself new
> and then return young and bright and dancing in the sky.

After either ritual, eat your meal. When you are done, one adult says:

> Dark time
> Quiet time
> Sleep time
> Dream time
> Time of change.
> Sleep well tonight
> with wonderful dreams.

Then put the moon candle back in the shrine, still wrapped in the dark cloth. One of the children can do this. Alternatively, you can keep the moon candle on the table till morning as a reminder of the dark time.

New Moon

The words "New Moon" can mean different things to different people. To some, they indicate the dark time, the moonless nights when the moon changes from waning to waxing. To others, they describe the first sliver of the waxing moon that shows itself just at sunset and disappears soon after.

The reappearance of the moon was celebrated by ancient Pagans more than the dark time was. Sometimes contests were held among villagers, the winner being the one who saw the moon first. The *Carmina Gadelica* (see resources) gives a number of beautiful Gaelic prayers for this day. It's a day well suited for family celebration, especially if you have a clear view of the place in the sky where the moon will reappear. If you can't find the moon on its first night because of intervening objects, light pollution, or bad weather, keep trying on subsequent nights until you succeed.

New Moon Ritual

Go outside right before sunset. In a city, you can use a balcony or a rooftop, or even an open window. (It's considered bad luck to see the moon first through glass.) Bring the wrapped moon candle with you. If you wish, make a braid from silver and/or white ribbons, attach it to a stick, and bring it outside with you. You could also decorate the stick with mirrors or silver jewelry.

Face west and watch for the sun to set and the moon to appear. (Don't look straight at the sun!) As the light fades, the moon will become visible just above where the sun set. The first one to see it gets to take the stick and point at the moon. (The adults can make sure this is one of the children.) The child then unwraps the moon candle and holds it up to the moon, saying:

> *She's back!*
> *Welcome back, Moon.*

The child puts both the stick and the candle down, and kisses their hand to the moon. Then everyone else does so. The candle and the stick are brought inside and put on the table. If they're old enough, the child who saw the moon first lights the moon candle. If not, an adult does. While the candle is being lit, the child who saw the moon first says:

> *The Moon is back*
> *and a New Moon begins.*
> *New things will happen.*

The mother, or another adult, says:

> *Think about it:*
> *What new things do you want to happen in the New Moon?*
> *What new things will you make happen in the New Moon?*

The members of the family can then say what they plan for the New Moon—or not, as they wish. (Remember: the embarrassment factor.) This is a good time to make vows. For instance: "I will meditate daily for this month."

If other Pagan families live near you, you can gather together for a contest. Whichever family sees the moon first gets to keep the moon stick till the next new moon.

For a less complicated New Moon observance, after everyone is at the table for dinner, one of the adults says:

> *Has anyone seen the moon tonight?*

If no one has, then everyone can go out to look for it. If more than one person has, you can compare the times to determine who saw it first. (This can become quite a competition.) Whoever sees the moon first gets to put the moon candle on the table and uncover it. If the child is old enough, let them light it; if not, have the mother or another adult do it. The winning child also gets to blow the candle out at the end of the meal.

For either ritual, put a bowl of olive or corn oil on the table. Hold it over the lit candle for a few seconds and then anoint each family member's forehead with it, saying:

> *May she be with you this month*
> *and smile on you every day.*

Full Moon

The Full Moon comes about every four weeks. The exact time can be found in almanacs, on many calendars, and online. Be careful to know the proper night and time. For example, if the Full Moon is on Tuesday at 3:30 AM, the night of the Full Moon is Monday. Calendars will frequently give the day as Tuesday, so you have to know the time as well as the day.

Because the Full Moon comes so often and is so important, it's good to have a variety of prayers for it. I give some examples below. The outline of the Full Moon ritual can stay the same from month to month, while the prayers change. The unchanging element in the ritual is the lighting and blessing of the moon candle, followed by a prayer.

Use your best dishes for this ritual and prepare a meal of light-colored lunar foods (almonds, cucumbers, seafood—especially shellfish or crustaceans—croissants, pita bread, white wine, milk, honey, water). Include moon cakes, which you can save for moon rituals to make them special.

Making Moon Cakes

Moon cakes can be just about any kind of light-colored cookie, although almond is a traditional flavoring. Here's one recipe:

> ¼ cup shortening
> ¼ cup butter
> ¾ cup sugar
> 1 oz. milk
> ½ tsp. vanilla
> ½ tsp. almond extract
> 2 cups flour
> 1½ tsp. baking powder

Preheat the oven to 350°. Cream the first three ingredients together. Add the remaining ingredients and blend with a wooden spoon. Roll the dough out ⅛" thick on a floured board and cut using a round cookie cutter. Then use the cutter to mark a crescent on the circles by cutting only part of the way through. Bake them for 8–9 minutes on an ungreased cookie sheet. Remove them from the cookie sheet promptly and let them cool.

Making a Moon Crown

Adult women should wear moon crowns when performing this ritual. Since this is a mark of the identification between women and the moon, at least in part through their monthly cycles, girls shouldn't wear these crowns until they come of age. Beautiful crowns made of silver or copper can be bought online, or you can make them from cloth.

To do this, cut two pieces of white felt in the shape shown in Figure 4. On one, outline the moon shapes with silver liquid embroidery. Cut two small vertical slits in the middle of the other, about ½" apart. I recommend reinforcing these with glue. After the glue is dry, thread a long blue or silver ribbon through the slits. The ribbon should be long enough to be tied around your head with plenty left over to hang down your back. Even out the ends of the ribbon and then glue the two felt pieces together. To wear the crown, tie the ends of the ribbon together behind your head and let the ends dangle.

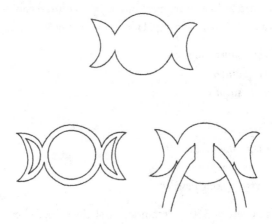

Figure 4. Steps for making a moon crown.

Full Moon Ritual

Place your moon candle in the middle of the table in a bowl, preferably of clear or blue glass. Make sure the bowl's big enough to hold the candle and some water. Fill the bowl with water. Set the table with your best dishes. When the meal's ready, establish sacred time and say a mealtime prayer (see chapter 6). When all is ready, a child says:

> *Why is tonight special?*

An adult answers:

> *Tonight is the Full Moon.*

The same child (or another one) says:

> *Why is that a special time?*

An adult answers:

> *The Full Moon is the Mother Time,*
> *time to be with family and friends,*
> *to celebrate all the wonderful things*
> *the Earth gives birth to.*

or

> *The Full Moon is our Mother*
> *Who wraps Her arms around us.*
> *She guards us and loves us*
> *and tonight we return that love.*

Of course, you can use another Full Moon prayer if you like. As in the Dark Moon ritual, the adults can ask the children the questions and let the children answer in their own words.

After these exchanges, the mother or another adult lights the moon candle and holds it above the table. Everyone says:

> *The Full Moon is shining, high in the sky.*

Then the mother or another adult returns the moon candle to the bowl of water, while everyone says:

> *The Full Moon is shining, here in our home.*

Everyone puts their hands over their hearts and says:

> *The Full Moon is shining, deep in our hearts.*

Then have your dinner. At the end of the meal, clear the table, leaving your glasses and the moon candle. Then set the table again with cakes and drinks. When ready, an adult says:

> *We share the gifts of the Full Moon with Her and each other*
> *on the night when She rides high in the sky.*

Pass the cakes and drinks around while one parent says:

> *Mother of us all,*
> *Watch over us.*
> *Hug us*
> *Hold us*
> *Wrap us round with your loving arms*
> *and keep us safe until the Moon is full again.*

(Everyone can repeat the lines ending with "us.")

After the mooncakes are eaten, blow out the moon candle and pour the melted wax from it into the water. It will cool quickly. Use the wax's shape to divine from, to see what the next month will bring. For young children, this can be a game of "What does it look like?" As the children go to bed, anoint each of them with the water, saying:

> *May the Moon send you good dreams.*

The moon water can also be used for sprinklings, offerings, or watering plants.

Full Moon Prayers

Here are some alternative prayers you can use, either after lighting the moon candle or while the cakes are being passed out:

Mother Moon
Watch over us
Mother Moon
Keep us safe
Mother Moon
Wrap us in your arms
Mother Moon
Shine brightly on our way.

♦ ♦ ♦

Mother of All, worthy of great honor,
watch over us as the month goes by
and bring us to the next Full Moon
safe and healthy and happy.

CHAPTER 8

The Changing Seasons

All religions have sacred days. What sets the Pagan holy days apart from those of other Western religions is that they don't celebrate historical events. They celebrate themselves. What's special about a Pagan holy day is that it is *this* day. Pagans live in the world and therefore find religious meaning in the events of the world. The most radical, and at the same time the most enduring, of these events are those concerned with seasonal change, and so Pagans build their lives around these changes and celebrate them as turning points.

Some have thought that ancient Pagans believed that without their rituals the seasons wouldn't change. Perhaps some did believe this. But what really matters for modern Pagans is that they and the world are changing in the same way. Whether there is cause and effect is irrelevant in this process. We do what we do because it's right for us to do it.

When we celebrate the festivals, we are honoring the seasons as we find them. We are recognizing them as sacred. But more than that, we are taking part in the continual creation of the universe. For us, the world isn't something created long ago and then fixed in place, but a continual unfolding of the sacred. The gods are continually giving birth to the world, and we are their midwives as well as their children.

The Wheel of the Year

As the seasons change, they turn the Wheel of the Year—a Neo-Pagan term for seasonal change when seen as a whole. Many Pagans have a particular form of the Wheel, expressed as a myth. These myths vary from group to group, but often contain elements in common: the birth of the sun, the marriage of the Goddess and the God, the death of the God, a battle between winter and summer, and the waxing and waning of the years. Other Pagans, especially Reconstructionists, see each festival day as special in itself, with no necessary relation to the other days. This was actually the most common view in ancient Paganism.

Whatever form of the myth is used (or none at all), however, the particular days celebrated by North American Neo-Pagans are generally those of Wicca. The Wiccan sacred calendar has eight holy days or festivals: Samhain (Halloween), Yule (the winter solstice), Imbolc (February 2nd), Ostara (the spring equinox), Beltane (May Day), Midsummer (the summer solstice), Lammas or Lugnasad (August Eve), and Harvest (the fall equinox). This calendar is sometimes described as Celtic, and there are indeed strong Celtic elements in it. The Gaels certainly celebrated four of these festivals—Samhain, Imbolc, Beltane, and Lugnasad. And, although the evidence for the other Celts is sketchy, they seem to have celebrated at least some of these four. The solstices and the equinoxes, on the other hand, came to Neo-Paganism from Germanic and Christian sources. Some modern Pagans have also added elements from Greece and the ancient Near East.

American Neo-Paganism has had many mothers, then, and more have been added since. That's one reason its festivals draw from many traditions, going beyond its British and European roots. In fact, they include customs from across the whole world. And for most Neo-Pagans, there's always room to draw from more. Although for most Neo-Pagans our ancestors are Indo-European and we're most comfortable with Indo-European ways, we know that, farther back in time, all people are one people and the wisdom of any may be appreciated by all.

Reconstructionist Pagans, on the other hand, usually use a festival calendar based on the culture in which they practice. Roman Pagans celebrate festivals like Terminalia and Parentalia, Greek Pagans celebrate Panathenaea and Anthesteria, Germanic Pagans celebrate the festivals of Thunar and Disting, Baltic Pagans celebrate Užgavėnės and Lyge, and so on. Because I don't have the space to include all (or even many) of these festivals, I've chosen to include rituals for two Roman holy days and otherwise limit myself to Wiccan celebrations. Some of these can be adapted to Reconstructionist holy days, though.

The rituals given below were written for a northern temperate climate, like the one in which the British Wheel of the Year developed. If you live in a different climate, please don't celebrate them on the traditional dates. Think about the meaning of each festival and choose a date that corresponds locally to that meaning. Remember, one of the points of being a Pagan is to be in tune with nature. That's hard to do if your calendar is out of whack.

I remember celebrating May Day in Gulfport, Mississippi, with a Maypole and ritual combat between winter and summer. There we were, celebrating the beginning of a season that had actually begun a month and a half earlier. It just didn't work. If you feel you *must* celebrate the traditional dates (and the solstices and equinoxes certainly deserve to be celebrated), change the rituals to reflect the seasons where you are. What's going on at your time and in your place? *That's* what you must celebrate.

A common mistake made in interpreting the seasonal customs of other cultures is to look at the date on the calendar instead of the seasons of the place where the customs originated. This has waylaid many, for instance, into thinking that the dying god of the ancient Near East (Tammuz, Adonis, et al.) was a god of spring. His festival does occur near the spring equinox, it's true, and there's much equinoctial symbolism in the god's myth and cult. But in the area where he was worshipped, the spring equinox is the time of the barley harvest, not the return of life after death and cold. Rituals inspired by this kind of myth would therefore be more appropriately celebrated in our fall season. For this reason, some of the suggestions for celebrating festivals taken from cultures in different climates have shifted away from their traditional calendar dates. Your rituals should reflect nature's calendar, not Pope Gregory's.

Look around you for other days that your family can celebrate in addition to the traditional seasonal festivals. My family has been known to celebrate baseball's opening day. (Well, the Yankees' opening day, to be precise.) If you live in a fishing community, what are the days that mark the rhythms of the ocean and the cycle of the catch? If you farm, when are your crops planted and harvested? Pagans who live in a community that relies on skiers for its livelihood might well celebrate the first snowfall. Paganism has a long history of supporting the economic well-being of its followers.

Think also about secular holidays (Valentine's Day, St. Patrick's Day, Memorial Day, the Fourth of July, Labor Day) that are near the traditional festivals. What can be incorporated from them into your own celebrations? Some non-Pagan celebrations in your community probably have a long history (harvest fairs, for instance), while others are more recent, like First Night celebrations. But these all represent responses by people to the seasons, so consider celebrating them in a Pagan way. They're part of our culture and reflect the turning of the year. Or just celebrate them in their secular form. You're part of a community most of which is non-Pagan, but forming strong community ties is a very Pagan thing to do. Giving to charity is also appropriate for several of these festivals. This can increase your bond with the community and establish the sort of social connection that was the reason for many of the rituals in the first place.

Few Neo-Pagans grew up in our religion. But we did grow up in a different kind of household. For most of us, this was a Christian one that did certain things on certain days. Some of these practices were Christian adaptations of Pagan customs. This isn't to say that all Christian holiday customs were taken from Paganism. But, as humans, we all share certain characteristics and, because of this, certain symbols will call to us all, no matter what religion they come from. And, since Christians can be as creative as Pagans, you have to keep in mind that some of these symbols and practices will have been invented by them, no matter how Pagan they may look. The local versions of these symbols will vary, but the truth behind them will not.

To see what these basic symbols are, think of your own childhood. I grew up as a Roman Catholic, so let me use that as an example. For me as a child, the biggest holiday was, of course, Christmas. When I think of Christmas, I think of decorations, foods, family gatherings, and presents. I don't think about ritual words. Emphasize those things in your own celebrations, then, the things you do, not the things you say. Think about your own childhood and what things were important to you about holidays and then incorporate these elements into your family celebrations.

Feasting, Festivity, and Fun

The most important element in ancient Pagan festivals seems to have been feasting. This should come as no surprise; since the material is sacred for a Pagan, eating is a sacred act, especially when done in the presence of the gods. An air of festivity surrounded ancient feasts, with decorations, games, and songs playing a central role. Were there rituals as well? Probably, but we usually don't know. There are certainly rituals in modern Pagan festivals, but they must never take the place of the feasting. Simply calling to the gods, feasting with them, and then having some fun can serve as a practice for any holy day.

The importance of traditional foods cannot be overemphasized. In my house when I was growing up, it just wouldn't have been Christmas without certain kinds of cookies. Children can help with food preparation, thereby learning useful skills while having fun celebrating the seasons.

Likewise, decorations both provide an air of festivity and act as a constant reminder of the significance and meaning of an occasion. Children can help make them and they can help put them up. You can find seasonal decorations that can be made by children in magazines and in teachers' resource books, and you can find instructional videos for many of them online. Making decorations is a great way to teach children the significance of sacred occasions.

Seasonal flowers are always appropriate as decorations; you can use the flowers that are in bloom at the time of your celebration. I can't give a list of flowers that would be appropriate for everywhere this book may be used, so you'll have to go out looking for them. Take your children with you so they can learn something about their local environment. You and your children can also grow flowers in your yard or in a window box, and you can also make a family activity out of gathering them from along roadsides.

And don't neglect weeds. Weeds are only plants growing where they're not wanted. A sure sign of spring is the dandelions brought home by schoolchildren everywhere as gifts for their parents. If you can gather wildflowers, you'll always be sure of having the right flowers for the season, and the change of them from festival to festival will reinforce the message of the seasonal change for your children. After the holiday is over, the flowers can either be left where they are until they've died completely (and then onto the compost heap with them), or you can place them in your shrine. In the winter, you can use bare sticks or evergreen branches. As one exception to the seasonal rule, you can cut branches with buds on them in the spring, bring them inside, and force the blossoms. You can even encourage your children to see this as a kind of magic to bring in the change of season.

Only necessary work should be done on festival days, which is standard practice for holidays in all cultures. In our predominantly Christian society, for instance, very little is open on Christmas. Similarly, in ancient Rome, no public business could be transacted on certain religious holidays. And in old Ireland, it was traditional to avoid all work that involved turning—spinning, driving carts, etc.—on holy days. But be sure to clean your house beforehand for the seasonal festivals, especially Samhain and Brigid's Day, when you invite others into your home. The effort expended in cleaning acts as an offering, and the clean house is a sign of respect toward your guests.

On the other hand, there's no ban on fun of any kind on these days. Besides rituals, food, and decorations, find fun things to do as a family. For all four of the solar festivals (the solstices and equinoxes) the traditional symbol is the wheel or the ball, the sun brought down to earth. So, depending on the season, try wiffle ball, bicycling, roller-skating, volleyball, sledding in plastic saucers, shooting marbles, bowling, or throwing disks. Go to an amusement park and ride the great wheels of light: the merry-go-rounds, the Ferris wheels, and those large drums that spin around so fast that you don't fall even when they tip (the ones my mother would never let me go on because she said they were too dangerous.)

Sacred Fire

Many of the seasonal rituals given in this book use fire: candles, bonfires, barbecue fires, even stoves and fireplaces. Fire plays a number of different roles in Paganism. Offerings can be made to (or through) the fire, a sort of sacrifice. You can give a portion of your own food and a bit of your own drink to the fire as a way to share a feast with a deity or spirit. The ashes from fires should be put on your garden if you have one to nourish the soil, or sprinkled around trees to bless and protect your home. (Ashes from barbecue briquettes shouldn't be used as fertilizer, though.)

Before having a bonfire, check with your local authorities to make sure it's allowed and safe. Some towns require permits for fires and, when conditions are dry, some towns don't allow them at all. Be sure the ground under the fire is free of anything that can burn, and clear an area around it as well. Surround the fire with a circle of rocks to retain and enclose the burning wood. Make sure you have buckets of water or sand or a fire extinguisher handy, in case the fire gets out of control.

When the fire is out, make sure it's *all* the way out before leaving it by soaking it with water, then stirring the ashes and soaking them again. Then check with your hand for hot spots. To do this, run your hand above the ashes (don't actually touch them), stir the ashes again and repeat. Don't leave any fire untended until you're sure it's out. Starting forest or brush fires won't make friends for Pagans, either with the spirits of the wild or with your neighbors.

Some of the rites given here are best performed on the eve of the day you are celebrating. In that case, the appropriate time can be considered to have begun the moment the first star can be seen. Alternatively, if you can see the horizon from your home, your family can watch the sun set before starting the ritual.

Making a Sun Candle

In chapter 7, I gave instructions on how to work with children to create a moon candle they can use in rituals that recognize the phases of the moon. Likewise, the rituals for the solar festivals often include the use of a sun candle, which serves to tie the solar and fire symbolism together. A solar candle is a large candle that's a solar color (red, yellow, orange, or gold). Since it's used in celebrations for four different festivals, it's best to use an unscented candle, because a scent that may fit perfectly with one festival may clash with another.

Children can decorate the base of these candles differently for each of the solar festivals—with holly for Yule (winter solstice), with flowers for Ostara (spring equinox), with leaves for Midsummer (summer solstice), and with fruit or grain for Harvest (fall equinox). Or you can help them cut an appropriate design into the candle with a hot knife. Keep the candle in your shrine when not in use.

Samhain

Samhain, or Halloween, is more closely associated with Paganism than any other holiday. It has preserved many Pagan customs and many more have grown up around it in Christian days. Indeed, unlike most Pagan occasions, there are almost too many customs associated with it to integrate them all easily.

The Irish name Samhain, pronounced "Sow-en" ("sow" like the pig), has been adopted by most American Neo-Pagans. The medieval Irish glossaries give its meaning as "summer's end," and that is its religious meaning among modern Pagans. Modern scholarship has cast some doubt on this etymology, however. One suggestion is that Samhain means "summer's beginning," the summer of the Underworld, where the seasons are the opposite of ours. What's beyond doubt, however, is that this day, which begins the cold part of the year, has summer in its name.

This is a good place to point out an error found in many books on Samhain that has unfortunately made its way into some parts of the

Pagan community. Samhain isn't the name of a Celtic god of the dead. There was no Celtic god named Samhain, or Samana as it's sometimes given. This error may have arisen from a confusion with Shamana, a title of Yama, the Vedic god of the dead. This name means "Settler" and isn't connected in any way with Samhain.

The term "Samhain" properly refers to the daylight portion of the festival, November 1st. The night of October 31st goes by a number of other names, including *Oíche na Sprideanna* (Spirit Night), *Oíche Shamhna* (Samhain Eve), and Púca Night. This is a night of magic, when fairies and ghosts are about, and the Púca spit on the blackberries, making them unfit to eat.

Among the Celts, as among the Hebrews and many others, the day began at sunset, with the dark time. The Celtic year also began with the dark, with Samhain. Just as a plant is born from the darkness below the ground, so too the year comes from the dark time. Samhain is thus the Celtic New Year's Day. If you work in a system with a different New Year's Day, consider transferring some of Samhain's customs to that day. For instance, Norse customs and myths surrounding the winter solstice are very similar to those surrounding Samhain. Roman customs for late February are similar as well, as the Romans were preparing for the new year that originally began in March, before it was changed to January.

The overwhelming cultural importance of the secular calendar has decreased the importance of the New Year aspect of Samhain for most Neo-Pagans. But if Samhain doesn't end the calendar year for us, it still marks the end of the year's growth. Not only does the world start to die at this time; it no longer puts forth new growth to replace death.

Samhain was the end of the farmer's year in temperate northern climates. Cattle and sheep were brought in from the far pastures, wood was all gathered in, and winter wheat already planted. Those of us who don't farm or even garden can use this time to wind up other things in our lives. For instance, debts can be paid if possible, to close the year so that the new year can begin free from connections to the old. Are there jobs around the house that you've been meaning to get to? Do them now, and free yourself to look forward instead of back.

The Wooing of Étaín, an early text of the Irish mythological cycle, tells us that, among the Irish, Samhain was a day of peace when no one could take up arms against another. This law is characteristic of tribal assemblies and, indeed, there's a slight possibility that the term Samhain actually means "assembly." Samhain is thus the great assembly day. If you're part of a Pagan group, gather them together for Samhain. If your extended family is Pagan, gather them as well. If you have no group with which to assemble, don't worry. The spirits of your ancestors will gather with you. This is one time when Pagans don't stand alone.

Samhain Customs

Samhain Eve is the night of death, when the fairy mounds open and the dead and the old gods walk the earth. On this night, gifts of food and drink are left out for them, in either appeasement or greeting. It's the night when the veil is thin between our world and that of the gods and spirits and anyone may pass through—in either direction. Many Samhain customs are designed to protect the home from these spirits or the fairies, although some Pagans welcome them, and so either don't keep some of these customs or reinterpret them. For instance, the jack-o'-lantern, far from scaring off spirits, may be seen as evidence of spirits in our midst.

In ancient Ireland, Samhain was actually part of a weeklong celebration that was divided into three parts: the three days before it, the day itself, and the three days after it. The feasting was long and well-celebrated. In remembrance of this, your celebration should extend for at least three days. That's why there are three rituals given here—one for the Night of Harvest's End, one for the Night of the Animal Spirits, and one for the Night of the Ancestors—each of which deals with a different aspect of Samhain. Unlike other festivals, where I give several rituals to choose from, all three of these are meant to be performed, one on each of three days. It's best to perform them on consecutive days, but, depending on local custom, you may have to reschedule one of them so as not to conflict with trick-or-treating.

The origin of trick-or-treating has been the subject of a lot of speculation, some of it based on evidence and some not. I wouldn't like to be the one more person saying "this is how it began." I don't think we can know for sure. We do know, though, that everywhere in the ancient world, the days before the New Year and feasts of the dead were a time of ritual chaos when the world dissolved, the cosmos disintegrated, and the human community allowed itself to fall apart as well. There were celebrations with costumes, general lawlessness, children's revolts, and trick-or-treating. The meaning seems to have been that with the old year dying and the new one not yet begun, the old rules were dead and the new ones not yet in place. It was thus a time for both fear and merrymaking.

We know that, in the British Isles, there are many customs associated with particular days that involve going from door to door collecting goodies: Pace Egging, Guy Fawkes, caroling, and, in areas influenced by the Gaels (or, in modern times, by Americans), Halloween. These customs died out in early America, but the influx of Irish immigrants during the Potato Famine was probably responsible for reviving them. This is conjecture, but the traditions are old, and probably pre-Christian.

Secular Halloween customs are therefore quite appropriate, and you can take part in them with a good conscience. As well as taking part in the local seasonal festivals, something that any self-respecting Pagan should be glad to do, and as well as giving your children a chance to feel that they're not that different from other children (something I'm sure most parents are glad to be able to do), you'll be observing the Festival of the Death of the Year in traditional fashion. Go for it.

If you're from a culture that reveres its ancestors, research its rites. If your culture already has a day for revering the ancestors, perhaps you should perform these rites on that day. And of course, when looking at cultures to derive customs from, don't forget our own, with its wreaths and flowers.

After the dissolution to chaos comes the recreation of the world. This is the origin of the belief in many parts of the world that what happens on New Year's sets the pattern for rest of the year. One offshoot of this belief is the custom of practicing divination on days like this. The pattern of a thing is set at its beginning, so the year's pattern can be seen or altered by divination on Samhain.

Each of the three rituals deals with a different aspect of the day. First there is the vegetal aspect. This is the time of the year when plants are dying; leaves fall from trees, the stems of wild flowers turn stiff and gray, and the plants in your garden are killed by the frost. On the second night is the placating of the spirits of the animals eaten during the year. This is a recognition that we live by killing. Being a vegetarian is no way out of this either. Life is life, and even vegetarians are responsible for death. In hunting cultures, it's common to placate the spirits of dead prey. This is partly to ensure their return and that they'll continue to cooperate in the business of living and dying. At least part of this custom, however, is based in a recognition that the animals also have spirits, and these spirits deserve respect. Animal death is specifically associated with Samhain.

In the days before electricity, some cultures even killed many of their domestic animals at this time. There was only so much fodder, and not all of the herds could be kept in good health until spring. Some of this meat was carefully preserved for the winter and some was used for a feast not unlike the American Thanksgiving. On Martinmas (November 11th, and thus Halloween in the old Julian calendar), farmers in Ireland killed an animal and sprinkled its blood on the threshold and the four corners for protection of the home. The meat was shared with the poor.

The third night is dedicated to honoring the Ancestors. It involves as well facing our personal mortality. While this aspect of the observance may not seem appropriate for a gathering with children, it's certain to be part of any meeting of adults or individual rites that may be held during this time.

The most effective way to schedule these rituals is to perform them in the order given here—first the ritual for plants, then for animals, then for people. This brings the message of Samhain closer to us personally each night. The celebration should reach its crescendo on the night of Samhain itself, with only visiting graves left. Even if your scheduling has to be different, be sure to leave the honoring of ancestors for the night of Samhain itself.

On one or more of the days of observance, it's appropriate to fast, except for the ritual feast. This custom is often associated with observances of New Year's days, as well as with preparations to meet with spirits. It also fits in with the coming of the hard times of winter when, in a subsistence culture, going without food might be a necessity. Since the central part of each day's observance is a meal, fasting will also give greater emphasis to that part of the ritual. If your family decides to fast, limit the fast to healthy, nonpregnant adults. Fasting will then be one of the responsibilities shared by those who have come of age.

Pagans spend so much energy thinking about nature that it would be all too easy to forget about the human community. So on Samhain, it's fitting to make a special act of charity, perhaps with the money saved by fasting. Samhain has always been a day for giving, a day when it's not proper to turn the stranger from your door. (Perhaps another theory of the origin of trick-or-treating, as Samhain is the perfect day to ask for gifts and know that they won't be refused.) It's the end of harvest, when our storehouses are full and we can certainly spare some of our goods. On Samhain, we call to the Ancestors and say: "Thank you for what you've done for us." And they reply: "And what have you done for each other? What have you done for your descendants?" If we are to face them without shame, we must have an answer.

Samhain is a time to clean your house particularly well. You'll be inviting the Ancestors in, and simple politeness requires a clean house. But more than this, Samhain ushers in a new year, and you should be able to face it with as little baggage from the old year as possible. In the same vein, you can wear new clothes for these rituals, especially for the Night of the Ancestors.

On the first day of the three, set up an extra table at one end of your kitchen or dining room table. Any size will do, as long as it is at least as high as your family table (and preferably higher). An end table will serve; you can set it on books or bricks if necessary to make it high enough. This table will serve as your Samhain altar, which will remain in place throughout the festival, decorated differently for each of the three days. Ordinarily your family table serves as your altar, but for this special day, a special altar is in order.

Celebrating Samhain

Decorations: Symbols of late fall, harvest, and death, like sickles, scythes, jack-o'-lanterns, skulls, skeletons, grave rubbings, root vegetables, squashes, and apples.

Food and drink: Dark food and foods that keep over the winter. Nuts, blackberries, apples, applecakes, applesauce, roots, squashes, beef, pork, dark bread, mulled cider or wine.

The Night of Harvest's End

Prepare a meal that emphasizes vegetables and fruits. Include a heavy dark bread—a dark rye or pumpernickel—unsliced. You and your family will eat from this loaf each night, so make sure there's some left over for the last night. Leave the loaf on the altar table for all three nights.

When the food is ready and the table set, gather the family together about it. After establishing sacred time, an adult says:

> *This is the first night of Samhain,*
> *The Night of Harvest's End.*
> *Summer is over and winter is upon us,*
> *the time to enjoy what our summer's work has earned us*
> *and the time to prepare for summer's return.*
> *Blessed be winter, this sacred time of the year.*

Everyone repeats the last line.

Go out to your garden. Stand right in the middle of it, facing west, the direction of the dying sun and of the journey made by the dead. Make one last offering to the spirits of the garden (beer or wine is appropriate) and say:

> *Goodbye, Summer.*
> *We have planted*
> *We have weeded*

We have harvested
We have watched the garden
and helped it grow
and now its end has come.

This is a good time for children to join in, thinking of things that have been done to help the garden and adding them to the list. If your children have their own garden(s), they should perform this part of the ritual by themselves there.

Then put the garden to sleep for the winter. Make the final harvest and pile the results in bowls. Pull up all the plants and haul them to your compost heap, then lay down mulch and compost. From some of the remains of the plants, make a figure of a man. This will be your image of winter. He'll rule over your household until May Day. If you don't have a garden, you can find weeds along the road or in a vacant lot and make your figure out of them. Use dead and dry weeds, especially those with seeds in them. The first year my family did this ritual, we didn't have a garden, so we used dried grass from a nearby vacant lot. You can also make the figure from wheat stalks, which can be bought in craft supply stores. In this case, you'll also need to procure bowls of fruits and vegetables, preferably from local farms.

To make the figure, make two bundles of stalks, one slightly thinner than the other, but both the same length. One and a half feet to two feet is a good size. Be sure to include some of each plant. The thinner bundle will be the arms. With a long piece of string, tie the large bundle together about one fourth of the way from one end (see Figure 5.) This will be the head end.

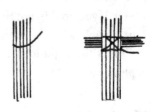

Figure 5. Making an image of winter.

Separate the bundle slightly below the string and insert the smaller bundle. Wrap the string diagonally across and around to hold the arms in place. Tie it off, leaving plenty of extra string. Then spread the lower portion of the large bundle apart to form the legs. Run the string down through the dividing point, back up to one arm and around it, then down to the dividing point again and back up to the other arm and around it. Pull the string tight to keep the legs divided and tie it off. You may also tie the ends of the bundles together. We like to keep ours rough, but you can make yours as elaborate as you like.

Bring the figure of winter into the house with ceremony and put it on the Samhain altar, propping it up so it can stand at its own place, with its own plate or bowl. You can also slip the string that ties the figure together over the top of a wine bottle to hold it up. Put your bowls of fruit and vegetables in front of the figure and put bits of your food on its plate or bowl as you eat, serving the figure first. Afterward, leave the food out for the spirits of the wild or of the garden. Face the figure of winter and say:

Welcome, Winter.

Keep Winter until Beltane. If you have enough privacy, you can put him in the garden on a pole in the north to watch over the garden for the winter. If you do this, put the offerings of food in front of the figure. You can also light a bonfire in the garden and carry fire around it to bless it.

This is the night for traditional Halloween games like bobbing for apples or trying to eat donuts that are suspended on strings.

The Night of the Animal Spirits

If you keep any animals (including pets), make sure that on this night no one eats dinner until they are fed. Leave out food for wild animals as well.

Your ritual meal should include a soup containing a little bit of every food animal you and your family have eaten during the year. Use any soup recipe with small pieces of the animals added. Beef stock works well as the base, because its strong flavor isn't easily overpowered by other meats. If you have difficulty including every type of animal consumed, beef traditionally stands for all animals, so it can be used by itself. If you're vegetarian, make a soup using as many plants as possible and adapt the ritual accordingly. When everything is ready, establish sacred time. Then an adult says:

> *This is the second night of Samhain,*
> *the Night of the Animal Spirits.*
> *This is the night when we thank the animals who have*
> *died for us.*
> *Blessed be the eaters.*
> *Blessed be the eaten.*
> *Blessed be the eating.*
> *Blessed be the being eaten.*
> *Blessed be life.*
> *Blessed be death.*

The other family members repeat each line beginning with "Blessed be" in a call-and-response fashion. Then the same adult or another says:

> *This is the great secret of life:*
> *That it feeds on death*
> *and they are close twins.*
> *The wheel is always turning.*
> *The spirits of the animals are here,*
> *of all that we have eaten.*
> *They have played their part in the turning of the wheel*
> *so tonight we do them honor.*
> *Thank you.*

Together or individually, each person, including the children, says "Thank you." Then one adult continues the prayer:

> *Thank you, animal spirits;*
> *we will not forget your gifts.*

Serve the soup, then eat your dinner, taking special care to taste and enjoy your food. Don't rush through the meal; that would be disrespectful to the animal spirits. Either make sure all the food is eaten or leave what's left over for the spirits. Whatever you do, don't waste any.

The Night of the Ancestors

The ancestors are who we are. Their genes live on in us; their culture shapes our days; their signs are all around us. The land itself speaks of them. Thus, on the night of Samhain itself—the Night of the Ancestors—it's only right that we should speak of them as well. Speak and remember, for what the ancestors desire most of us, what we most need to do, is to remember them.

The ancestors have often been ignored by Neo-Pagans. Perhaps that's because we've been enraptured by the Celts and have associated ancestor religion with Africa, China, and Japan. Maybe it's because so many of us have seen our path as breaking away from our family's religion. Or maybe it's just that Wicca lacks an emphasis on the ancestors. It is indeed ironic that those who seek to revive the ways of our ancestors have thought so rarely of the Way of the Ancestors. If you're from a culture that reveres its ancestors, research its rites. If your culture already has a day for revering the ancestors, perhaps you should perform these rites on that day. And of course, when exploring other cultures, don't forget your own.

The meal on this night should include pork, the sacred feast animal of northern Europe, and the food of the dead, apples, fruit of the tree that grows in the Otherworld. There will also be the dark bread that has been on the table for the first two nights.

Decorate the room with symbols of your ancestors, such as family trees and heirlooms. These need not be anything fancy. A letter, a piece of clothing, a book—anything from any ancestor. (One of my favorite heirlooms is a hammer my grandfather used.) Other possibilities include photographs of ancestors, or rubbings or photographs of gravestones. Flags, postcards, foods, statues, books, or other items from the countries of your ancestors are also appropriate.

Dress in dark clothes. This is the night of the Underworld, the night-time world. Ordinarily, we live in the daylight world, but on this night, we enter the world of darkness. The nighttime world is the world of mystery, just like the world of death. We cannot see what comes to us out of the dark.

This ritual is a case where a cluttered altar is called for. Many fore-bears have poured themselves into us and the result is a complicated culture filled with complicated people. Make your altar just as complicated. Raid your heirlooms and the traditions of your ancestors' cultures for tools, jewelry, and clothes. Put images that represent your ancestors on the altar. If your household guardians are figures of your ancestors, use them. Or you can use masks made just for this rite, jack-o'-lanterns, or other ethnic symbols. Place a candle on the altar for each relative who has died since last Samhain, plus an extra candle for all of your other ancestors. You can also put electric candles in the window to show the spirits the way to your home.

Place a plate before the ancestors on which you can serve the meal you will offer them. Put the candles for the dead in front of the ancestral images. As you light each one, say that person's name. These candles should be lit by whoever in the family was closest to the person. After the candles are lit, the oldest adult present says:

> Tonight is the last night of Samhain, the Night
>   of the Ancestors.
> It is the feast of dark bread.
> It is the feast of apples.
> It is the feast of pork.
> On this night
> we welcome the spirits of our ancestors.
> On this night
> we welcome you to our house.
> We share our meal with you who have given us so much.

Before serving any family members, put a bit of every kind of food at the meal on the ancestors' plate.

After the meal, clear the table, except for the plate of the ancestors. Put an apple, a pomegranate, a sharp knife, and a cup of cider on the table. The cider can be served mulled but cold by soaking cloves and cinnamon sticks in it overnight. Before pouring the cider, stir or shake it to mix the flavors, then strain out the spices. Pass the cup around, either counterclockwise (thereby going down to death) or from youngest to oldest (thereby approaching the ancestors). Whichever order you choose, make sure the cup ends up at the place of the ancestors.

As each person receives the cup, they recite their genealogy—women and girls in the female line and men and boys in the male line—saying:

> *I am ( ), the child of ( ), the child of ( ).*

Go as far back as your knowledge will take you or as far as you wish. Include at least one ancestor who is dead. If you don't know the names of your ancestors, say: "child of an ancestor unknown." Or perhaps, after a certain point in time, the names of your ancestors are lost to you. In this case, call them by what you do know. Identify them by where they came from, or by what their trade was, or by their relationship to you. There are many of my ancestors about whom I know nothing except a name. That isn't really much, but it's enough.

When done speaking, each person drinks a toast in the direction of the place of the ancestors. When everyone has spoken and the drink is at the place of the ancestors, one participant says:

> *We offer the cup of fellowship to the Ancestors.*
> *They are dead but not gone.*
> *We are all one people and tonight we eat and drink together*
> *   once more.*

Someone else says:

> *We are not the first*
> *We will not be the last*
> *We are not the river's source*
> *nor are we its end.*

Life flows on from the Ancestors
through us and beyond.
Daily we are carried along as life streams on.
Tonight we turn and look upstream
and honor our source
before turning again and plunging once more into life.
Tonight we remember our Ancestors:
Gone but remembered
Left but revered
Away but near our hearts.
Those who are remembered are still alive.
Those we remember are with us still.
We speak their names and remember.

(It's nice if the first four lines and the lines beginning with "Gone but remembered" are repeated by everyone in a call-and-response fashion.

And now comes the important part. *Remember.* Say the names of important ancestors and after each name tell some of what you know about them. Name those who have died since last Samhain first. It's alright to call out the names of friends as well as family. We are one people. Speak their names and remember them. When there are no more to remember, the oldest adult present says:

Ancestors going back into the darkness,
forgotten by history,
your lives unrecorded:
You who are unknown to us but who made us ourselves.
Don't be afraid:
You are not forgotten.
We remember you.

Everyone replies:

We remember you.

Then sit and remember. Don't be afraid to cry. Your tears will be an offering to the ancestors. And don't be ashamed *not* to cry. The remembering may bring you comfort without grief. When the remembering is done, the oldest adult present says:

> *Every day we will remember and every night when we sleep.*
> *We will always remember and we will never forget.*
> *These are our people and we remember them.*

If you have any messages you want to send to your ancestors, especially ones you don't want to say out loud, write them down on a piece of paper. Put the paper with incense on a burning piece of charcoal, or burn it in the flames of the candles of the ancestors. The smoke will take your messages to the ancestors for you. When all the talk is done and all the messages sent, the oldest adult says:

> *The table of remembering is over, but the Night of the*
> *Ancestors goes on.*
> *But there is one thing more we still have to do.*
> *For three days, we have spoken of death:*
> *of plants, of animals, of our ancestors.*
> *But our way is life.*

The oldest adult picks up the pomegranate, saying:

> *This is a fruit of life.*
> *It is filled with many seeds.*
> *But it was just these seeds that kept Persephone in the land*
> *of the dead.*
> *So what does this fruit say to us?*
> *It is life, whose shadow is death.*

The same adult cuts open the pomegranate, then holds up the apple, saying:

> *This is a fruit of death.*
> *It grows in the Otherworld where our ancestors live,*

> *where they are rested and refreshed,*
> *which is thus called the Land of Apples.*

The oldest adult cuts the apple through the middle horizontally and holds it up to show the star formed by the seed chambers, saying:

> *But hidden inside is the star of rebirth.*
> *So what does this fruit say to us?*
> *It is death, whose shadow is life and promises rebirth.*

The same adult holds up both fruits, saying:

> *Which is our way?*
> *Which path are we on?*
> *Are we on the path of death?*
> *Or are we on the path of life?*

All respond:

> *We are on the path of life.*

The oldest adult puts the fruits down, then puts the apple back together and puts it on the ancestors' plate, saying:

> *And this is your path:*
> *Death, with the promise of rebirth.*
> *We say goodbye to you for now*
> *as you go your way and we go ours.*

Blow out the candles and share the pomegranate.

Samhain was one of the great bonfire days of the Gaels. Any of the festivals may be celebrated outside with a bonfire, and the Night of Remembering is particularly appropriate for its inside equivalent, the fire in the fireplace, where you may gather after the meal for more stories of the ancestors. On the first night, you might also light a bonfire in the garden or fields and carry fire around them to bless them.

Save the apple and the offerings on the ancestors' plate for the next day. The day of Samhain is as magical as the night; the door between the worlds is still open. On this day, visit a cemetery. If possible, visit one where actual ancestors of yours are buried. If you can't do this, find the oldest cemetery possible. Walk through it, reading some of the names on the tombstones out loud. Try to imagine who these people were. If your ancestors are buried there, point out their graves to your children and explain who they were and how they're related. Leave offerings, including the apple and the food from the ancestors' plate, on some of the older graves, especially those of your actual ancestors. Say:

> We remember you, all our Ancestors.
> See, here we are;
> We have not forgotten you.
> See, here are our gifts.
> We have not been idle.
> We have not wasted what you have left us.

Any offerings you give in addition to the food from the previous night will depend on the culture you and they come from. In most cases, some sort of bread and drink will be right. A common gift in Indo-European cultures is beans. Seeds of all sorts are appropriate as promises of rebirth. If you visit the graves of your own relatives, you can leave offerings of their favorite foods or drawings made by your children.

Soulcakes

What sort of foods do you want to share with your ancestors? What kind do you think they'll like? Many cultures used what the British call "soulcakes"—small loaves made from the local grain. In India, these are made of rice, while the Ainu of northern Japan use millet cakes. In parts of the British Isles, they were basically pancakes. In parts of Russia, gingerbread was used. The most traditional soulcake, therefore, is whatever bread, cake, or cookie you eat for special occasions—whether pancakes, crêpes, corn bread, pita bread, biscuits, or Irish soda bread.

Ask yourself what sort of cakes you want to share with your ancestors? What kind do you think they'll like?

For a sweet soulcake with only three ingredients, try this easy-to-make shortbread. You'll need:

> *4 oz. (1 stick) unsalted butter, softened*
> *3 tbs. sugar*
> *1½ cups flour*

Preheat the oven to 375°. Cream the butter and sugar together in a bowl, then sift the flour into the bowl and work it into the butter and sugar until smooth. Divide the dough in half and shape each half into a circle about ½" thick. Put them on an ungreased cookie sheet. Cut partially through each circle into eight pieces and decorate them with fork marks. Bake for 10 minutes, then lower the heat to 325° and bake for another 20 minutes. Cool.

Soulcakes were often given to the poor as an expression of sharing the final harvest's bounty. They were also given to children who came to the door, perhaps yet another possible origin for trick-or-treating. Either practice may be a substitute for giving to the dead. In modern times, since the poor don't usually come to your door, you can leave baskets of food anonymously, or donate food or money to a food bank, or, even better, give some of your time to a soup kitchen.

Yule

Yule is the winter solstice, which, because the calendar year and the solar year aren't exactly the same, can be on different days in different years. However, it always occurs on or near December 21st, and most calendars or almanacs will give the exact day and time. You may want to celebrate it on December 25th, though, and why not; the rest of the country (or most of it, anyway) is already celebrating.

The word "solstice" means "the sun stands still." Since Midsummer, the sun has been rising and setting farther and farther south, thus appearing lower in the sky and for a shorter time each day. This led the ancients to wonder if this will continue. Will the Earth grow darker and colder as the sun disappears into the south until only darkness is left? In our heads, we know the light will return. But in the dark of winter, can we be sure? Do our hearts believe what our heads tell us? Will the light keep its promises? We all have moments of darkness when we don't know how much deeper we'll go before the light starts to return (or even if it will).

But on Yule, something wonderful happens. The sun stops its decline and, for a few days, it rises in approximately the same place. This is a crucial time, the cusp between events. The sun stands still, and everyone waits for the turning.

And then the sun *does* start north again and the light comes back. In the world, in our lives, the light comes back. This is indeed something worth celebrating, and it's been celebrated throughout the northern hemisphere in remarkably similar ways.

The most important part of celebrations around the time of the solstice has been light, in all its forms—Yule logs, bonfires, Christmas trees, Kwanzaa candles, menorahs. The meaning of the lights varies from culture to culture, and even from person to person. They can be magic to help the sun's return, a sign of hope in the dark and cold, a symbol of the Unconquerable Sun to cheer us, or a festival multiplication of the necessary lights of dark times. But then, Paganism is a religion of doing, not believing, so what matters isn't how you *see* the light, it's what you *do* about it. Bring back the light in your home and know that it will also be coming back into the world.

The word "Yule," according to The Venerable Bede, means "wheel." We don't know whether the term was meant to refer to the wheel of the sun or the turning of the Wheel of the Year, but either meaning would be appropriate. It apparently meant the entire season—the last month of one year and the first month of the next. Most recently scholars have been less certain of its derivation and have been more likely to give its origin as simply "Germanic, original meaning unknown." Regardless of its original meaning, however, "Yule" is a short, friendly word that fits well into our language. It's familiar even to non-Pagans through songs, originally written for Christmas, that use it and that can be adopted by Pagans. In fact, many Christmas customs are derived from more ancient

Yule customs. The Christmas tree, the Yule log, wreaths, lights, and fires all have their origin in Pagan Midwinter customs.

Yet as we have them, these customs are definitely Christian. The Christmas tree as we know it was not put up by the Pagans of old. It's true that northern Europeans decorated their homes with pine boughs and that Romans hung trees with masks and fruit in honor of the new year. Still, the modern Christmas tree is the result of years of development within a Christian framework. Because of this, some Pagans may prefer to skip the custom altogether, especially those who grew up as non-Christians. Some may wish to return to a simpler, more Pagan version of the practice. On the other hand, others may choose to adopt the whole package of modern customs, even those that have no ties to Paganism whatsoever, giving suitable thanks to Christians for their creativity. There's no reason why these symbols of life in death and light out of darkness can't be used by both by Christians and Pagans.

Yule Trees

If you do use a tree in your Yule celebration, make a big deal out of it. Put it up in the afternoon of Yule and leave it up either for twelve days (one for each month, and also to tie in with medieval Twelfth Night customs) or until Imbolc. (Or, if you use a cut tree, until the needles start to fall off.)

Whether you use a cut tree, a live tree that you can plant in the spring, or an artificial tree is a personal decision. Pagans can use any of these in good conscience. A live tree is perhaps the best, but we don't all have the luxury of owning land to plant one on. Cut trees are grown on farms, so if they are disposed of responsibly, Pagans should feel no worse about using one than about eating a carrot. Many communities collect trees for mulching or erosion control, or you can take yours into the woods where it will provide shelter for small animals. Pagans aren't overly fond of plastic, but artificial trees, which can last for years, are entirely appropriate to use. In fact, if a member of your family has allergies, it may be your only choice.

Many decorations for Yule trees are commercially available or can easily be made at home. You can use small masks like the Romans who hung masks of Bacchus on trees for Saturnalia, their Midwinter feast. You can string cranberries (solar symbols) and popcorn for garlands that can be put outside later for the birds. Roosters, horses, golden balls and discs, candles, oranges, flame-colored ribbons and streamers, wheels, chariots, lights, wreaths, six-pointed stars, dragons, phoenixes, eagles, hawks, lions—all are sun symbols appropriate to Yule. In stores, you can find simple colored balls made in the sun colors of red, gold, yellow, and orange, as well as figures of elves and fairies. And don't forget the symbols of winter—white balls, icicles, and snowflakes. And when it comes right down to it, there's nothing wrong with using an ornament just because you think it's pretty.

One thing my family does is to run gold-colored garlands from the lamp over our dining room table to the tops of our windows and doors, and suspend sun symbols from them. Over the years, I've collected quite a few sun ornaments and mixed them in with gold-colored balls. This creates what I call a "solar canopy" and it's quite striking. When we turn on the light, the room seems to glow.

Prepare a meal for the afternoon, one that's light enough to leave room for feasting later and doesn't take much time to make. Soup, salad, and melted cheese on bread is enough. For a special treat, toast pita bread (white or whole wheat) under the broiler and cover it with sliced toma-toes. Then broil it again and top it with cheddar cheese sprinkled with chopped basil. Broil it again until the cheese melts. These are messy to eat, but good, and full of solar symbolism. The round bread, the golden cheese, and the red wheels of tomato make up your own suns on earth. For drinks, serve cranberry juice, orange juice, or eggnog. Cranberry juice is good served hot, especially with clove and cinnamon added.

When the tree is set up in its stand and the decorations are ready to hang, gather around it with a bowl of water and an asperser made of evergreen branches. An adult says:

> *The Spirit of Growth is here in our house,*
> *here in the midst of winter,*

to tell us to wait with hope and with longing
for the sun's return
and green's rebirth.

Sprinkle the tree and each other, and then decorate the tree. You can turn on the lights momentarily to test them, but don't leave them on longer than necessary until after the Yule feast and the Yule-night ritual.

Celebrating Yule

Decorations: Candles, lights of all kinds, evergreens, roosters, suns, holly and ivy, mistletoe (a plant so Pagan it was banned from churches). Make "luminarias" by filling paper bags partway with sand and placing a lit candle in the sand. The candle shines through with a golden-brown glow, perfect for Yule.

Food and drink: Anything round, golden, or hot. Shortbread, fruitcake, eggnog, mulled wine, cranberry juice, orange juice, corn bread baked in a round pan, oranges, gingerbread, chicken, and suet pudding, commonly called plum pudding.

Plum Pudding

Although it wasn't originally a Pagan dish, plum pudding is a popular Yuletide treat. Oddly, it doesn't have any plums in it. It's often served with brandy poured over it and lit, making it a burning wheel and thus a perfect symbol of Yule. Here's my family's recipe:

> *3 cups flour*
> *1 cup ground suet*
> *1 cup raisins or currants*
> *1 tsp. baking soda*
> *1 tsp. cinnamon*
> *½ tsp. ground clove*
> *¼ tsp. nutmeg*
> *1 tsp. salt*

1 cup molasses
1 cup milk

Mix everything together and put into a greased deep round pan. (The kind with a separate side and bottom is best.) Fill the pan only half full. Cover it tightly with foil and put it on a rack in a large pot. Fill the pot with water halfway up the sides of the pan. Steam for three hours, adding water as necessary. When cool, remove the pudding from the pan, wrap it in foil, and put it in the refrigerator or freezer. This has to be made at least a month in advance to allow the flavors to mellow. (Trust me; it tastes lousy if you don't do this.)

To reheat, thaw the pudding and heat slices in a microwave. Serve them with flaming brandy or hard sauce (butter with enough confectioners' sugar in it to make it stiff; you can also add vanilla extract).

Yule Feast

After decorating the tree, but before turning its lights on, eat your evening meal. Use your best dishes and have appropriate foods like shortbread, fruitcake, eggnog, corn bread baked in a round pan, oranges, gingerbread, chicken, plum pudding, or any other culturally traditional Midwinter and festival foods. Roast boar—most of us will use pork—is a traditional Germanic Yule food.

After your meal, clear the table, wash and dry the dishes, and put them away. Then take as many candles as possible and put them in holders. You can use saucers and bowls if you run out of candlesticks. Just melt some wax onto each dish and stick a candle in it before the wax hardens. You may want to do this earlier in the day, as it can take some time. Put all these candles on the table, with your sun candle in the middle. Then turn off every light in the house.

The ritual extinguishing and relighting of fires is found in many traditions. The day on which it's done varies, but Yule is a popular time. Although we no longer have a central hearth with a fire that burns continuously, we do have furnaces that can be turned off early in the day and then turned back on as part of the ritual.

When everyone is seated and the house is dark, an adult says:

For half the year, day by day,
slowly the world has grown darker.
For half the year, night by night,
slowly the dark has grown longer.
Tonight that ends and the wheel turns.
Our land turns back to the light.

Everyone can repeat "day by day" and "night by night" in a call-and-response fashion. When you are ready, light the sun candle and say:

The darkness was never complete
A spark was always waiting,
to return and turn again.
And now it will grow greater and greater.
The light will come back.
The cold will go away.
And once more we will dance in the warmth
until the wheel turns again.
It has always been this way,
The wheel turning from darkness to light and back again
and our people have always known this and have
*   turned with it.*

All say:

The wheel is turning and light's returning.

An adult starts a litany. The response to each line is: "Light is reborn." With each answer, one more candle is lit, until they're all burning. The lines of the litany can go something like this:

In the greatest darkness
*   (Response: "Light is reborn.")*
Out of winter's cold
*   (Response: "Light is reborn.")*

From our deepest fears
   (Response: "Light is reborn.")
When we most despair
   (Response: "Light is reborn.")
When all seems lost
   (Response: "Light is reborn.")
When the earth lies waste
   (Response: "Light is reborn.")
When animals hide
   (Response: "Light is reborn.")
When the river is frozen
   (Response: "Light is reborn.")
When the ground is hard
   (Response: "Light is reborn.")
From the midst of the wasteland
   (Response: "Light is reborn.")
When hope is gone
   (Response: "Light is reborn.")
Out from the hard times
   (Response: "Light is reborn.")

These lines can be said by different people taking turns, and can even be made up on the spot. Continue in this way until half the candles are lit. Then change the emphasis of the litany to something like this:

Shadows are fleeing.
   (Response: "Light is reborn.")
Light is returning.
   (Response: "Light is reborn.")
Warmth will come again.
   (Response: "Light is reborn.")
Summer will be here once more.
   (Response: "Light is reborn.")
Plants will grow again.
   (Response: "Light is reborn.")

Animals will be seen once more.
> *(Response: "Light is reborn.")*

Life will continue.
> *(Response: "Light is reborn.")*

Green will come again.
> *(Response: "Light is reborn.")*

Darkness will not last forever.
> *(Response: "Light is reborn.")*

Continue until all the candles are lit. Then take a deep breath and bask in the candlelight for just a moment. Then run through the house (carry small children) and turn on every light. Running is important to add a touch of festivity and abandon. (Be sure to leave an adult behind to stay with the candles.) Don't forget closets, attics, stoves, flashlights, and even cellphones. If you have lights for decorations on a Yule tree or outside, turn them on now. If you have turned off your furnace, turn it back on. You will find that children are quite good at finding lights you have forgotten.

When all the lights are on, return to the table. Sit in the glow for a while, eating, drinking, and talking. This is one of my favorite moments of the year. I can feel the light throbbing through the walls of my home. For a family normally obsessed with turning off unneeded lights, this is a special moment indeed. The feeling stays with me for days.

Bring out the cookies and eggnog and have some fun. Then slowly go through the house again, turning the lights back off. Blow out all the candles except for the sun candle; leave that burning until you have to go to bed. Relight it first thing in the morning and leave it burning all day if you can. Burn it each day as long as the tree is up.

You may want to celebrate this ritual at dawn instead. If you've adopted the Christian custom of putting presents under the tree, there's a good chance your children will be getting up at dawn anyway. Just light your sun candle again and say:

The sun is back.
He is born again.

Then open your presents and eat breakfast.

Wassail Blessing

It was (and I hope still is) traditional in some parts of England to bless the fruit trees at this time of year. People made a bowl of a spiced ale drink called wassail, then drank some and sprinkled the trees with it, crying out: "Waes-hail!" ("Be whole!") This was accompanied by loud noises, including the firing of guns.

To make wassail, heat (but don't boil) ale with chopped fresh ginger added. Use about ½" of fresh ginger for each bottle of ale. While the ale is heating, core one apple for each bottle of ale and bake at 350° until soft. Add them to the ale when it's ready. When the ale is warm enough and has picked up enough ginger flavor, strain it and sweeten it to taste.

For a nonalcoholic version of wassail that your children can drink too, you can use cider or ginger beer. If you use cider, make sure it doesn't boil, or it will separate. Although children won't be able to drink the alcoholic wassail, they can certainly shout, sprinkle, and make loud noises.

Imbolc

This celebration has many names. In Gaelic, it is called *Imbolc* (the "b" is silent) and *Oimelc*. The medieval Irish glossaries give the meaning of *Oimelc* as "ewe's milk." Modern scholars are not so sure, but suggest instead that *Imbolc* is to be related to a word for bag, full belly, or womb. English Christians call it Candlemas, while the Romans called it Lupercalia. Anglo-Celtic tradition calls it Brigid's Day. And to many Neo-Pagans, it's known as Lady's Day, although some use that name for Beltane or Ostara instead.

All these names show some of the meanings of the day. Imbolc is basically a precursor to spring. In the gentle climate of Ireland, warmed by the Gulf Stream, it is considered the first day of spring, marking the time when lambs are born, ewes lactate, candles are blessed, Brigid, Lady of Fire, returns, and the hedgehog pokes its head out of the earth. In the climate of northern America, however, winter is only half over.

The Gaelic sagas are silent about Imbolc's significance, and it's not even mentioned in non-Gaelic Celtic traditions, but it's a day it's easy to find references to folk traditions for. In America, it's commonly known as Groundhog Day. This tradition originated from the belief that, if it was fair on Imbolc, winter would continue; if it was foul, winter was over. In Ireland, the decision was made by the hedgehog, an animal with many a role in folklore, but in hedgehogless America, this role was taken over by the groundhog.

From the Roman Lupercalia and the Christian Candlemas comes a theme of purification. In Rome, a goat was sacrificed outside the city on February 15th and two men, dressed only in a thong made from its hide, ran through Rome, striking people as they went with thongs also made from the goatskin. It was considered especially fortunate for women to be struck. The Romans themselves didn't know the meaning of this ritual, but thought it had to do with fertility and purification in anticipation of the spring sowing. In fact, the Latin *Februa* appears to have a meaning connected with purification.

Candlemas, on the other hand, is a purely Christian feast. Jewish law required that women be ritually purified on a certain day after childbirth, a custom that survived into Christian times as the "churching" of women. With the birth of Jesus set on December 25, the time for Mary's purification would have fallen on February 2nd. The association with candles isn't from a Pagan source, but comes rather from Luke 2:32, where Simeon says that Jesus will be "a light for revelation to the Gentiles."

Some Wiccan traditions believe that Imbolc represents the purification (the "revirginization," if you will) of the Goddess after the birth of the sun god. While this is great poetry and makes for a fine myth, it must be remembered that it's a modern interpretation inspired by Christian practice rather than by ancient Pagan belief.

No matter the source, the theme of purification is best suited to warmer climates as a preparation for sowing. Pagans living in such a climate might wish to emphasize that. But those living in cooler climates might prefer to emphasize the midpoint of winter. Up here in New England, for instance, we have something called "January Thaw," a period of a week or two when the temperature rises and some of the snow melts. When I was in high school, the snow in my yard was always the last on the street to melt in the spring. We took advantage of January Thaw to shovel some of it onto the snow-warmed driveway and sidewalk, where it would melt, leaving that much less for the spring. One peculiar thing about January Thaw is that it frequently comes in the first week of February. If your area has a similar weather event, consider celebrating Imbolc then.

Celebrating Imbolc

Decorations: bells, fire, candles, a sun, flowers, running water, or anything else that means spring to you.

Food: Dairy products, sprouts, fruitcakes (maybe you can finally finish that last bit of Yule fruitcake), lamb.

Ritual of Melting

Prepare a collection of small bells (jingle bells will do fine), one set for each person. Go outside with them, with a small candle like a birthday candle, matches, and an empty bowl. Draw a symbol of spring in the snow. This could be fire, a sun, a flower, running water, or anything else that means spring to you. Your children can help decide on which symbols to use, or they can each draw one of their own if they want. Ring the bells to symbolize the melting of ice and snow, and say:

> *The snow will melt and spring will come again.*

Put the candle in the middle of the symbol, light it, and say:

> *Here in the snow, a spark of spring is growing.*

Fill the bowl with snow and bring it inside, ringing the bells as you go. Leave the candle to burn out. Place the bowl on the table and have your holiday meal. At the end of the meal, an adult holds up the now-melted snow (it's okay to cheat a little and put it somewhere extra warm) and says:

> The snow may lie deep

Everyone responds:

> but the melting time will come.

The adult says:

> The water may still be hard ice

Everyone answers:

> but the time will come for it to flow.

While the bells are rung again, the adult pours the water into another bowl, saying:

> See, it's true—
> winter won't last forever!
> The sun is indeed growing strong and bringing back
> the warmth.
> The snow will melt and the earth grow green again.

Then everyone rings their bells again and whoops it up. You can use the water to bless the family members or to water a plant.

Brigid's Day

Under the name of "Brigid's Day" Imbolc is a living festival in Ireland. The Irish, of course, have a strong history of blending the Old Ways with Catholicism and, in their Brigid's Day celebrations, they have most likely preserved many customs from Pagan days.

The Irish goddess Brigid (or Brighid, Bride, or Brigit, traditionally pronounced like "breed," but now often pronounced like the name Bridget) became the Catholic Saint Bridget. She is a multifaceted (or multiple) goddess of poetry, smithing, healing, fire, and spring. Her name means "the high or exalted one." From this, and from her multiple functions, it's obvious that she's a very great goddess. Her fire associations are shown in the forge of the smith, the inspiration of the poet, and the life heat of the healer. In the folk tradition from which the ritual below comes, she's worn down some (as deities tend to do), and now her fire burns on the hearth, where she serves as the guardian of the home. She is thus a partial equivalent of Hestia or Vesta; she watches over all energy in a house and protects the house from danger, especially from fire.

Brigid is the patroness of all who work with cows, and all who deal in dairy products. She travels the world with her red-eared white cow and is especially likely to come to visit on her day. Offerings are left out for Brigid and her cow, and then taken by the poor in her name. This is therefore a traditional day for giving charity, especially food, and especially to the homeless.

If you celebrate this ritual, you will have called Brigid as your hearth guardian. If you have an affinity with a different hearth guardian, use that spirit's name and symbol in the ritual or perform a different ritual—for instance, Vestalia.

Making a Brigid's Cross

For the ritual, you will need a Brigid's Cross, and making one is a traditional part of the events of the day. These take different forms in different parts of Ireland. The most common and simplest of these is essentially a God's Eye made of two sticks and straw (see chapter 5). The best-known, however, in America at least, is an off-center cross, as shown in Figure 6. The legends of Saint Bridget say she wove the first one while explaining Christianity to her father, but it's possible that the symbol is pre-Christian.

Many Neo-Pagans consider the Brigid's Cross to be a fire wheel, which certainly explains its characteristic off-center shape, but this description doesn't fit the other forms of the cross, so we'll just have to leave its origin a mystery.

In old Ireland, most homes had a central hearth over which the Brigid's Cross was hung. The hearth was the source of the household's warmth, cooking, light, and hot water. When more than one cross was made, they were hung in other places in the home as well. Indeed, in some parts of Ireland Brigid's Crosses were drawn on people and walls with charcoal as a mark of protection. Although modern homes have several different devices that can be called hearths, it's more common to hang one cross over the stove rather than to hang several crosses. You can draw crosses on the other hearths with charcoal. If you have several children and they each make a cross, you can string them together and hang them in one place. The crosses are said to protect a home from lightning, fire, and storm, and to protect family members against illness.

Figure 6. A Brigid's Cross with the characteristic off-center arms.

You can find Brigid's Crosses in Irish craft stores or online. Even brass ones can be bought, like the one that decorates our front door. It's customary to burn the cross each year and make a new one, to start fresh, although some not only make a new one, but keep the old ones somewhere, such as in the rafters. It you can't find a Brigid's Cross, don't worry; you can easily make one from reeds, straw, wheat stalks, or construction paper. If you're using dry reeds or straw, soak the materials overnight to soften them. Some reeds won't soften enough, so you'll want to experiment by yourself before trying this with children. The arms of the cross can be of any convenient length.

To start, bend two pieces of reed or straw in the middle to form loops. Link them together as shown in figure 7, then turn the pieces so they lie flat and form a right angle. This is the only time in the construction when the pieces will be hooked through each other like this. This two-piece construction will form the base of the cross.

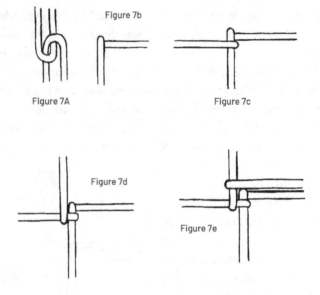

Figure 7. Instructions for making a Brigid's Cross.

Next, bend another piece of reed or straw in half and loop it over one of the two base pieces, passing both legs of the loop over both legs of the base. Pull the reed tight and hold it in place. Then bend another piece of reed or straw and loop it over the two legs of the last piece you put on. Continue doing this until the cross is the size you want. Tie the ends together with string, reed, or straw and trim.

Brigid's Day Ritual

First set the table with your best dishes. Prepare the food for the meal, but don't cook it yet.

Among the food, include a loaf of bread in the shape of a Brigid's Cross using any bread recipe you prefer. After the last rising, divide the dough in fourths. Shape each piece into a long roll and fold it in half. Hook the pieces together to make a simple Brigid's Cross, squeezing the tips in the center together. You can bake the bread the day before or later in the ritual when you cook the rest of the food.

When everything is ready, a woman or girl from the family takes the role of Brigid, going outside with a Brigid's Cross and a lit candle in a jar or oil lamp. She knocks on the door (leave it open a crack so the rest of the family can hear her), and says:

> *Brigid is here, to bless this house.*
> *Open the door, and let her in.*

After Brigid has done this three times, those inside open the door and say:

> *Lady Brigid,*
> *come in, come in, come in.*
> *Welcome to our house.*
> *You are thrice welcome.*

Brigid enters and holds up the candle and cross. The others say:

> *Lady of Fire,*
> *Burn in our hearts.*
> *Bring the Spring.*

Brigid then passes the cross over the flame, saying:

> *May the blessing of Brigid be on this cross*
> *and on the place where it hangs*
> *and on all who see it*
> *through all the year.*

If the weather is too bad, just put the cross outside near the door, with the lit candle or oil lamp next to it. Try to do this without being caught by any of your children. When everyone's ready, welcome Brigid and open the door. Bring in the cross and candle and continue with the ritual as written. You can also do this if there's no woman or girl present to play the role of Brigid (or a male child can play her part).

One family member takes the candle and another takes the cross, and together they lead the rest of the family through every room in the house. A child can carry the cross. If you have more than one child, they can take turns, changing when you go from one room to another. In each room, hold up the cross and candle while someone or everyone says:

> Brigid, Lady of Fire,
> Watch over this room.

Mark Brigid's Crosses on your water heater, furnace, and fireplaces or woodstoves with charcoal as you come to them. You can bring incense with you as well—pine is appropriate for Brigid, as it burns fast and hot. The needles of your Yule tree or of a wreath are perfect for this. Go to your kitchen last. Hang the cross over the stove, and say:

> Brigid, Queen of the Hearth,
> Keep us safe,
> Keep us warm,
> Extend your blessing over this our home.

After the cross is hung, turn on the oven to start cooking your food. Put the lit candle on the table and let it burn until the meal is over. Spend the time waiting for the food to cook doing something as a family. Since Brigid is a goddess of making things, crafts are an appropriate activity.

After dinner, the person who was Brigid at the door (or an adult if you didn't have someone at the door) says:

> Brigid will shine in our house through the whole year.

Everyone says:

> Blessings to our Lady Brigid.

Brigid then blows out the fire.

Terminalia

Terminalia is the festival of the Roman god Terminus, god of the boundary stone. Terminalia could fall on either February 23rd or March 1st, putting it at or near the beginning of the old Roman year. The celebration appears to have been moved to the end of December when January 1st became the New Year, though, and since that's also when our year starts, it may make sense to celebrate Terminalia between Yule and the first day of January, when offerings to Janus, god of the threshold, are made. This creates a natural progression from a day dedicated to the god of the borders to one dedicated to the god of the threshold.

In the climate of northern Europe and northern America, however, none of these dates may be practical. It may be too cold, and the border marker dedicated to Terminus may well be under snow. If that's the case, choose another day. Since Terminus is associated with boundaries of time as well as space, you might choose a day associated with your household: the date you moved in and honored Terminus for the first time on your land, for instance. Whatever day you choose, Terminalia is a festival for families to celebrate, even for those who don't practice in the Roman tradition, since all homes have boundaries.

Celebrating Terminalia

For this ritual, you will need a garland or wreath, a lit candle in a jar, sweet wine, grain (flour or pearled barley is fine), and honey (a honeycomb if possible). Dress in white clothes (a white shirt will be enough.)

Go to your boundary marker and establish sacred time. Put the candle on top of or next to the maker, saying:

> *We establish the fire of offering.*

Put the garland on or around the marker, saying:

> *Be honored, Terminus (or the name of your border deity if*
> *you have a different one, or simply, "God/Goddess of the*
> *Border" if yours is unnamed),*
> *with the garland of victory,*
> *with the garland of peace:*
> *bring protection and peace to those who dwell on your land*

and to all who enter as guests
and to all we own.

Hold the wine over the fire for a few moments, then pour it around the boundary marker, saying:

We offer in return sweet wine,
filled with spirit,
filled with life:
fill us with spirit and life.

Hold the grain over the fire a few moments, and then cast it on the border marker, saying:

We offer in return grain,
food of our bodies,
food of our strength:
fill our bodies with strength.

Pour or place the honey on the border marker, saying:

We offer in return honey,
source of sweetness,
source of happiness:
fill us with sweetness and happiness.

Then say:

You are strong, Terminus
You are faithful, Terminus
and so on this day we praise and offer to you,
well-deserved praise, well-deserved offerings,
and well-deserved thanks
for bringing protection and peace to our property
and to all who live on it
and to all who enter as guests.
We ask that you continue to do so in the year ahead.

Be strong, Terminus
Be faithful, Terminus
and on each Terminalia we will praise and offer to you.

The prayers and offerings can be split up among members of the family as you wish. It's traditional for the mother to bring the fire, a son to offer the grain, and a daughter to offer the honey, but these roles can be played by any family member as well.

Ostara

Imbolc brings the promise of new warmth and light. But it isn't until Ostara that the light is equal to the darkness. For Ostara is the spring equinox—the "equal night." After Ostara, there can be no doubt. The tide has definitely turned and the light half of the year has begun.

Ostara is also known as Eoster. It's ironic that Easter, the English name for the holiest day in the Christian calendar, should have a Pagan origin. But Bede relates the Christian name to Eostre, the Germanic goddess of spring. Although there is some doubt that a such a goddess actually existed, the name Eostre definitely comes from the Indo-European *Aus(t)ro*, from the root *aus*, meaning "to rise." Johann Knobloch has theorized that the Germanic word therefore originally meant "dawn" (see Robbins, p. 202). Ostara is thus the dawn of the year.

One point that must be made here is that Easter is not related to either Ishtar or Astarte. The names of these Goddesses are Semitic, not Indo-European. It's true, however, that some of the myths and rituals of these goddesses are sympathetic to Ostara and may be incorporated into its celebration if you remove all harvest associations.

Although the festival's name is Germanic, we don't know if German Pagans actually celebrated the spring equinox. It may have been celebrated in northern Europe in Neolithic times, but in the historical period it shows up first as being introduced by the Romans. The Pagan Celts didn't celebrate the equinoxes at all, so the next infusion into the north was by Christians.

In southern Europe and the ancient Near East, however, things were different. Among many of the peoples there—the Romans and Babylonians, for instance—the spring equinox was the beginning of the new year. The Roman calendar even originally had a gap between the end of December and the spring equinox. When the equinox came around, the agricultural year started again. As mentioned earlier, in the ancient Near East, the spring equinox was the time of the barley harvest. If you want to include customs from that area in your Ostara celebration, then, be careful to distinguish customs appropriate to planting and sowing from those of the harvest.

Since the Celts didn't celebrate Ostara, there's some overlap between it and other Celtic festivals. If you'd like, you can see Ostara as either the culmination of Imbolc or a precursor to Beltane. Alternatively you can put the main emphasis on the day's solar or astrological significance.

The secular customs that surround Easter aren't exactly Christian, but they may not be specifically Pagan either. Eggs are obvious symbols of new life, and the flamboyant mating of rabbits and hares at this time ("mad as a March hare") make these animals appropriate symbols as well. Some of these symbols may have been invented by Christians, but only as natural associations with the seasons rather than as developments of the Christian message. Many of them are certainly found in Pagan cultures, so most secular Easter customs can be adopted wholeheartedly by Neo-Pagans. Colored eggs, baskets, jelly beans, candy rabbits, and flowers—use them all. Chocolate bunnies may not be of Pagan origin, but who cares?

If you have a garden, Ostara is a good day to plant it if you live in an area where the threat of frost is past. If you live in a colder climate, plant seeds inside in peat pots on this day and then transplant them outside on May Day. When you plant your garden, be sure to leave part of your yard for the spirits of the wild. Give them offerings each year before planting. If you don't have a good relationship with the wild, you have no business planting a garden.

It's good for Pagans to be involved in the production of at least part of their own food. This is an easy way to be involved in the cycle of life and death. If you have no space for a yard, you should still find a nearby patch of wild land and cultivate a relationship with it.

On Ostara, go fly a kite. It's March, after all, the month of wind. Make it a bright yellow kite with ribbons hanging from it, or one in the shape of a solar hawk or eagle. Use your best dishes. Put your sun candle in the center of the table with early spring flowers around it, if any have already bloomed.

In the first ritual below, Ostara is treated as a precursor of Beltane. The ritual thus predicts and invokes warmth and acknowledges the beginning of spring. The second ritual marks the fulfillment of Imbolc: winter is over, and the snow and ice are melting. Both rituals work with the solar symbolism that's the hallmark of the day.

Celebrating Ostara

Decorations: Suns, wind socks, leaves, new flowers (especially yellow ones like daffodils or forsythia), pussy willows. The foliage can be used to bless, either by using it as an asperser or simply by passing it around among family members. Anything yellow or green, especially spring green. Rabbits, eggs.

Food: Solar foods—chicken; red, yellow, and orange side dishes; and eggs. Quiche is also good, being round, golden, and made of eggs. To relieve the monotony, include a salad with strong green colors and sprouts in it.

Waking Up Spring

Prepare an outdoor fire, either a bonfire or in a barbecue. Gather around it in daylight with noisemakers. These can be drums set right on the ground; if there's snow on the ground, set them on something to protect them. You can also use rattles, horns, and any of the little noisemakers sold for parties. The father, or another parent figure, takes the role of the sun. He holds up the sun candle and a lighter, and says:

We are here to wake up the spring.

The person in the sun role lights the candle and holds it up to the sun, then, from it, lights the fire (using an intermediary taper or match), saying:

> Here in front of us the fire leaps up,
> leaping from us up to the sky
> up to where the sun is shining,
> the shining sun in the sky looking down
> looking down here where our fire is burning.
> Fire of the Sun,
> Burn in our midst.
> Fire of the Sun,
> Burn in our midst.
> Fire of the Spring,
> Burn in our midst.
> Warm us and the world as the season turns to spring.

Everyone joins in with the words "burn in our midst." Then everyone makes noise using their noisemakers and pounding on the ground or the drums. While they do this, they repeat:

> Wake up, Earth.

Continue the noisemaking until you want to stop. If it's warm enough, you can stay outside around the fire. If not, go inside for a meal.

Welcoming the Sun's Return

During the day, boil thirteen eggs as a family. If there are a large number of people in your family, boil twenty-five eggs. Dye all but one of them sun colors (red, yellow, and orange). Leave one white. You can do this on the day before your celebration if time is a problem. At dinner, put the eggs in a bowl next to the sun candle in the middle of your table, with the white egg on the top of the pile. The eggs represent one or two suns for each month of the year, plus one winter egg.

After sacred time is established, a family member—either an adult or a child—picks up the white egg and bangs it on the table to crack it, then removes the shell, saying:

> *The ice cracks.*

They remove the white, saying:

> *The snow melts.*

They hold up the yolk, saying:

> *The Sun is coming back.*
> *And now that he is armed*
> *and now that he is strong*
> *He will chase away the cold,*
> *he will bring us spring*
> *and summer is sure to follow.*

Pass around the pieces of the egg for everyone to share before starting the rest of the meal. Eat the colored eggs with the meal. You can reserve one for an offering if you like.

Egg Fights

An Easter tradition practiced in many places that's fun here (especially if your version of the Wheel of the Year puts the beginning of the battle between winter and spring at the spring equinox) is egg fights.

Each person chooses an egg. Two people then face the small ends of their eggs pointing toward each other and one of them hits the other's egg with their own. When one person's egg cracks, they turn theirs around and have another chance with the other side. When both ends of an egg are cracked, that person is out. The game continues until one egg is triumphant.

In my family, we write a name on each egg before fighting—people, significant places, schools, sports teams, etc.

Save the colored shells till Beltane and use them to decorate your May tree or bush (see below).

Beltane

May Day, called Beltane ("bright fire") by the Gaels, is the great day of celebration in Europe, from Ireland to Russia. Finally, the weather is warm. Winter is officially over. In Ireland, it was the day that the cattle were sent to their summer pastures.

Beltane is halfway around from Samhain on the Wheel of the Year, and they're similar in many ways. Both are days when the veil is thin between the worlds, both are bonfire days, both mark a halfway point in the year. In Welsh legend, Beltane is the most common day for supernatural happenings, just as Samhain is in Ireland.

In Scotland, Beltane celebrations once lasted for eight days, with the first and the last being especially important. This made the festival one day longer than Samhain, perhaps to make the time celebrating life longer than the time that celebrated death.

Beltane may have gotten its name from the solar god Bel, whose name survives in Latinized forms like Belenus and is completely unrelated to the Semitic god's name Ba'al. The day is strongly associated with bonfires. In Celtic times, cattle were driven between two bonfires on Beltane to protect them before they were sent out to pasture. People would jump over the fires, both as a blessing and for the sheer fun or sport of it. (If you do this, please be careful not to wear loose-fitting clothes, and don't push yourself to see who can jump the farthest or over the highest flames.) For a couple to jump over a Beltane fire together was as good as an announcement of betrothal. In the first ritual below, the bonfire is replaced with a barbecue, but if you can have a bonfire, do so.

Beltane is a day that deserves our full celebration. Take the day off; take the kids out of school; go on a picnic. Play outdoor games; throw around a ball; have a game of tag; run races; play croquet. Archery is particularly associated with this day, being found in both England (where of course it was connected with Robin Hood) and Germany.

May Day as we know it is a combination of the Celtic Beltane, with its bonfires and rowan, and the Roman Floralia, with its May Queen and flowers, although the Roman elements have come to predominate, as shown by a list of a typical European May Day celebration (Leach, pp. 695–696):

- The gathering of green branches and flowers on May Eve or very early May Day morning.

- The choosing and crowning of a May Queen (and often a king as well) who goes singing from door to door carrying flowers or a May tree, soliciting donations in return for the "blessing of the May." If you do this, the May King or Queen should be accompanied by other children. I don't see it working these days, though, unless it's turned into a neighborhood thing. Perhaps it can be described as trying to revive old May Day traditions. Don't do this unless your neighbors want to join in, though. The May Queen was seen by the English as representing the Roman goddess Flora.

- The erection and decoration of a May tree or bush, or Maypole.

For family celebrations, decorate a tree or bush in your yard with ribbons, flowers, and the eggshells saved from Ostara, then perform your May rituals around it. Consider this bush or tree to be the family version of a Maypole. Dance around it, just as you would any Maypole. For gatherings larger than a family, erect a Maypole hung with ribbons and dance around it, weaving the ribbons around the pole. Any kind of music, even current pop songs, is fine.

You can also use large indoor plants like ficus trees for May bushes. Or you can decorate decks, balconies, or windows. We decorate our garden each summer with ribbons in the colors of the elements. We buy new ribbons each year and add the old ones to our supply for next spring's May Day, which we tie to the fence around our deck.

Leave cloths out on Beltane Eve to soak up the dew, or leave out cookie sheets to collect it. (Although cloth is traditional, cookie sheets work better.) This dew can then be used for a variety of purposes. Washing with it is said to make the skin beautiful, and it makes a good base for herbal brews.

Oddly enough, there is a Roman holiday that is even more similar to Beltane than Floralia. This was Parilia, celebrated on April 27th, and intended to increase the fertility and milk production of the herds. As described in Ovid's *Fasti*, the animals' stalls were swept and decorated with foliage. Cakes, milk, and meat were offered to the pastoral deity Pales (or deities; the Romans didn't know whether Pales was singular or plural, or even a god or a goddess). The flocks were then driven through fires and blessed with the smoke, and the people washed their hands in dew, drank milk and wine, and jumped three times over the fires toward the east.

What makes this festival particularly interesting to us here is the date on which it was celebrated. Since the climate in Rome is milder than in the British Isles, it's only to be expected that the Romans would celebrate a festival similar to Beltane earlier than the Celts. And here it is: flocks driven through bonfires and people purified in dew. The custom of jumping over bonfires at this time of the year was also practiced in Armenia, adopted from an Iranian custom. This shows that Beltane was a widespread celebration of this season, observed across many cultures.

If your children are older, and especially if there are other Pagans in your area, get them up very early on Beltane or let them stay up very late on Beltane Eve to gather greens to decorate each others' doors. Rowan was traditionally used for these decorations, although any greenery and flowers will do. Make sure you do this in time for the decorations to be discovered by the sun.

Beltane Eve is winter's last hurrah. One last night for winter to rule, and then he dies. Six months earlier, the figure of Winter to help celebrate Samhain was made and fêted; now do it once more and drink toasts and make offerings to him and the turning of the Year.

CELEBRATING BELTANE

Decorations: Flowers, ribbons, rowan branches, branches with new leaves or buds, wreaths of flowers. Decorate your shrine with flowers.

Food and drink: May wine, a sweet wine flavored with woodruff that can be bought already prepared or made at home; place strawberry halves in the glasses if you can. Green food, especially fresh mint. Violets—both the flowers and the leaves can be eaten, and the flowers look interesting in a salad.

Lighting the Fire of Summer

May Day, the great day of picnics, is a perfect day for a barbecue. If this is your first barbecue of the season, prepare the grill by removing all the ashes from last year to start a new season. You want the fire to blaze up, so be sure to use lots of lighter fluid. Practice conservation some other time; May Day is all about excess.

The parts assigned to the May Queen in this ritual may be performed by any of the women or older girls present. You can choose the queen by lot, using marbles drawn from a box, or you can roll dice or draw cards. Crown the woman or girl chosen with a wreath of flowers or leaves before the ritual.

Put matches, lighter fluid, the figure of Winter, a pot, and a bucket or bowl of water (for fire safety) next to the barbecue. The pot can be either a cauldron that you use in coven or personal rituals, or one you use for cooking. Either way, it has to be large enough for the figure of Winter to fit into it. When everything is ready, gather about the barbecue. The May Queen says:

> *The Wheel of the Year has been turning.*
> *The fire of spring has been burning.*
> *The fire and the wheel have brought us here to May Day,*
> *beginning of summer.*

> *It's time now to light the fire of summer,*
> *to burn away all that remains of winter.*

Then the father lights the barbecue. (Give it one more squirt of lighter fluid first.) When the flames have died down some, the May Queen takes the figure of Winter and lights it from the flames, then puts it into the pot or cauldron to finish burning. If your backyard is private enough or the neighbors sufficiently understanding, do the burning (or perhaps the whole ritual) in the garden itself. While Winter burns, say:

> *Winter is gone and summer is here.*
> *Winter is dead and summer is alive.*
> *Winter is ashes in summer's green earth.*

Fan the smoke so it blows on each person present as a blessing. When the figure of Winter is completely burned, scatter the ashes in the garden. Dig a hole earlier in the day deep enough to hold any remains in case Winter hasn't burned completely. (If your figure is made out of dead grass, this is likely.) If you don't have a garden, you can scatter the ashes in a local wild spot or in a friend's garden. As you bury or scatter them, say:

> *From the ashes of winter*
> *Summer springs up:*
> *Green and bright and shining and warm.*

Throughout the year, save nail clippings and hair trimmings (including stubble cleaned from electric razors) in a bag. After scattering the ashes, scatter the hair and nails and work them into the soil, saying:

> *From the Earth to us*
> *From us to the Earth*
> *The wheel is always turning.*

Then barbecue. Spare ribs are particularly good; the sacred pig—bright red, spicy hot, and messy—is the perfect food for this celebration.

The next day, transplant the plants in your peat pots outside and prepare the rest of your garden.

Banishing Summer's Troubles

This ritual is adopted from a Scottish Beltane ritual recorded in 1769 by Thomas Pennant. It can be interwoven with the first ritual or done on its own. It can also be done by people who have nowhere to plant a garden.

Bake a round loaf of bread using the grain most commonly eaten in your area. If you live in an agricultural region, use the grain that's grown there. Bring the loaf to a wild spot that's as close to your house as you can find, or just your backyard. Stand in a circle and pass the bread around, each person breaking off a piece as it comes to them. When everyone has a piece, someone says:

> *All beings of the air who stand in opposition to us,*
> *eagles and hawks, who carry away our animals,*
> *starlings who eat our seeds,*
> *crows who eat our dead:*
> *here is your part of the offering;*
> *don't trouble us.*

All throw their piece of bread over their left shoulder with their left hand, saying:

> *Don't trouble us.*

Pass the bread around again, with each person again breaking off a piece. The person who spoke first (or someone else) says:

> *All beings of the earth who stand in opposition to us,*
> *wolves and coyotes who carry off our animals,*
> *rabbits and deer who eat our gardens,*
> *ants and termites who destroy our homes:*

here is your part of the offering;
don't trouble us.

Everyone throws their piece of bread over their left shoulder with their left hand, saying:

Don't trouble us.

Pass the bread around again, with each person again breaking off a piece. Then person who spoke first (or someone else) says:

All beings of the Underworld and water
who stand in opposition to us,
bacteria and viruses that carry away our health,
sharks and jellyfish that drive us from the ocean,
grubs and beetles that feed on our food:
here is your part of the offering;
don't trouble us.

Everyone throws their piece of bread over their left shoulder with their left hand, saying:

Don't trouble us.

Pass the bread around again, with each person again breaking off a piece. Then person who spoke first (or someone else) says:

All beings of air, earth, and water
who stand in opposition to us:
we have given you your part of the offering;
don't trouble us!

Everyone throws their piece of bread over their left shoulder with their left hand, saying:

Don't trouble us!

You can move a few steps to one side each time everyone says "don't trouble us," if you want, so people can throw their bread in different directions. When the ritual is complete, go back to the house or out to a restaurant for a good, fancy meal.

When I wrote this ritual, I intended it to be solemn. But when my grove performed it, they laughed each time they threw a piece of bread. The first year I was kind of ticked off by this. But then I figured that they knew better than me. Expect similar jollity on this day of celebration. Besides, laughter is said to be a good way to banish.

Ambarvalia

This Roman festival is similar to the circumambulation of property described in chapter 3. It can be seen, in fact, as a repetition or strengthening of that ritual. It was usually celebrated around agricultural land but is also appropriate for a household.

Because it involved a purification of the fields where crops grew and an invocation of deities for protection and fertility, it's likely this celebration was connected to a particular point in the agricultural year, perhaps the time of planting or the time of sprouting. Ambarvalia was eventually assigned to May 29th, but, because of its association with seasonal change, it likely started out as a movable feast. Because of this, it can be celebrated either on May 29th or on any day associated with a stage in your garden's growth or your household, such as the anniversary of moving into your home. It can also be celebrated as an extension of Terminalia, acknowledging first the border stone and then the land boundaries that the stone and god define.

Because of a description provided by Cato in *On Agriculture*, with additional details from the poets Virgil and Tibullus, we have a detailed account of this holiday, which is rare for ancient traditions. The ritual described here is based loosely on these sources, adapted for modern times and simplified.

A major part of the original ritual was the circumambulation of the land with a pig, a sheep, and a bull, all of which were eventually sacrificed. Since sacrificing live animals isn't acceptable in modern times, these animals are replaced here with either breads or cakes baked in the shapes of the animals. The identity of these with the animals relies on the declaration of them as such. Make the breads or cakes a size that you can conveniently carry, and make sure you have enough for everyone, with some left over for offerings. Depending on how big you make them, you can put them all on one plate, or they can go on separate plates. You'll also need a bowl of water with which to purify the family, the animals, and your land, as well as a bowl of grain or flour and some wine. Make sure you have enough water and flour in your bowls to purify everyone present. Dress in white (white shirts are enough), and preferably wear a wreath made of oak leaves.

The spoken parts can be broken up among those present. Children can do the pouring and sprinkling.

Blessing the Borders and the Land

Gather together by the marker of your border guardian and establish sacred time. Someone says:

> *We pray together at the festival of Ambarvalia,*
> *that we, our home, our guests, our property, and all that*
> *grows on it*
> *will be purified and protected.*

Someone pours out the wine, saving some for later, and says:

> *Father Mars, be our protector*
> *from all disease, accidents, and failure of food,*
> *that all may prosper*
> *for which we make offerings to you,*
> *an expiation of pig and sheep and bull.*

With the last three lines, they (or someone else) hold up the plate of breads or cakes or hold their hands over them. Someone then sprinkles the animals with water, saying:

> *With the pure, we will purify.*

Someone sprinkles the animals with grain or flour, saying:

> *With the blessed, we will bless.*

Then carry the animals and the bowls of water and grain around the border of your land, occasionally sprinkling some water and grain, particularly on prominent features like impressive trees and stones. Make sure you sprinkle some at the corners. At these spots, present the animals, saying:

> *[Name of feature], we are purifying this land with water*
> > *and grain.*
> *and with this pig and sheep and bull,*
> *as was done by the ancestors.*

When you return to the boundary marker, sprinkle it with water and grain. Present the animals again using the same words. Then someone says:

> *Terminus, who guards our lands,*
> *to you we pour out this libation.*

They pour out the remaining grain, and then someone says:

> *To you we scatter this grain.*

After the grain is scattered, someone says:

> *and to you we pray for protection.*

Then someone else holds up the animals, saying:

Father Mars, great protector,
we offer you these animals,
which we have led about our land.
Bless it with them which we offer to you.
With pig,

Someone breaks off a piece of the pig, then breaks that into smaller pieces and scatters it around. The speaker says:

With sheep,

Someone breaks off a piece of the sheep, then breaks that into smaller pieces, and scatters it around. The speaker says:

With bull.

Someone breaks off a piece of the bull, then breaks that into smaller pieces, and scatters it around. The speaker says:

We offer you this prayer.

Then pass the plate(s) of animals around, each person breaking off a piece of each animal. When everyone has their pieces, they hold them up and someone says:

We share a meal with you.
Be ever our guest.
Be ever our host.

Finally, everyone eats their pieces of bread or cake.

Then go back into your home and have a feast. Eat the rest of the breads or cakes as part of this. If there's too much left to finish, leave it in your shrine for twenty-four hours and then offer it to the spirits of the land, saying:

To the spirits, the leavings.

Midsummer

Midsummer, the summer solstice, is the high point of the sun. At no other time will it rise so far in the north or be so high at noon. What started at Yule now reaches its completion. The European traditions universally used both bonfires and water in their Midsummer celebrations. Wheels covered in straw were lit on fire and rolled down hills to land in a pond, or were thrown directly into water. Bonfires were lit on hilltops. Saint John's Day (June 23rd) is celebrated with bonfires in many places to this day, especially in Ireland and Norway.

It may be the direct opposition of fire and water that makes them attractive for Midsummer celebrations. Although it's the day on which the sun is at its strongest, Midsummer is also the day on which it starts to weaken. Then again, maybe the purpose isn't so much to celebrate the sun's power, but to mitigate its heat. The intent may also be to prevent drought during a crucial growing season by subordinating the sun wheel to water.

Midsummer celebrations therefore call for bonfires if possible. If you can't build a bonfire, you can substitute a barbecue. A good time to perform a barbecue ritual is at noon, the high point of the sun, but a bonfire should be lit at sunset so it will show up better in the dark.

To include water in your celebrations while having fun with your children, try playing with it. You can swim, run through sprinklers, have water fights. And it's hard to beat the fun and symbolism of sun-colored water balloons. And I do mean *you*; why let the children have all the fun? (And they'll have even more fun if you participate with them.) This is a good day to establish a tradition of going to the beach.

The first two rituals given below use an asperser. One way to make this is to tie a bunch of Saint John's wort together with a gold ribbon. This herb derives its name from the fact that it blooms around June 23rd, which is Saint John's Day in the Catholic calendar. After the ritual, hang the asperser in your home. Saint John's wort is said to protect the house from lightning. If this herb doesn't bloom around this day in your area, instead use a flower that does, preferably a red or yellow one, or daisies ("day's eyes").

Midsummer Fire Ritual

Once again your barbecue serves as a substitute bonfire. Pour lots of charcoal and soak it with lighter fluid. Put the grate back on the barbecue and place a pot of water on it. You can use the same pot you used for the May Day ritual, but be careful not to use one with plastic handles, as they can melt. Put the lighter fluid, matches or a lighter, and an asperser nearby.

When everything is ready and everyone is gathered around the barbecue, establish sacred time. Then the father (or the oldest adult male present) says:

> Today the Wheel has come to a special point.
> Since Yule, the light has been growing.
> At Ostara, the light became greater than the dark
> and it kept on growing.
> It has grown until today,
> Midsummer, the middle of the light time.
> Tomorrow, the light will start to fade as the Wheel
>   turns to darkness
> until it is Yule again.
> But today it is bright.
> Today the sun is high.
> Today the world is filled with light
> and we celebrate this with fire.

The sun blazes above.
Our fire blazes below.

Everyone repeats these last two lines:

The sun blazes above.
Our fire blazes below.

You can replace the words "the sun" with the name of a solar deity.

With the line "our fire blazes below," add one more squirt of lighter fluid and light the fire. When the flames have died down a bit, have each person take the asperser, dip it in the water, and sprinkle the others with it. (Alternatively, each person can have their own asperser.) Then remove the pot from the grill and, after it cools, water your garden or a tree with the water. When the coals are ready, barbecue. Waiting for the coals to be ready is a good time for playing with water.

Midsummer Water Ritual

This ritual is meant to be performed on a beach. If you are lucky enough to live near the ocean, that would be a perfect place for it. If not, a lake or pond is fine. It can also be (and has been) performed quite satisfactorily indoors with a bowl of water.

You'll need a sand pail, a candle (preferably one in a jar to keep it from being blown out), something to sprinkle water with, and a lighter. Start the ritual at noon. Go down to the edge of the water, fill the pail, and then bring it back up the beach. Somewhere in between the high and low tide marks is best. That's the in-between place, neither land nor water, and is thus especially sacred. Light the candle, hold it up, and say:

The sun is high on the longest day.

Lower the candle to the surface of the water and say:

Starting today it starts to get darker
as the sun goes into the water.

Submerge the candle and say:

> *The sun goes into the water,*
> *blesses it,*
> *and fertilizes it.*

Use the water to sprinkle to the four quarters, saying:

> *The waters of life flow to all directions of the Earth*

Sprinkle each other, saying:

> *and bless all who live on it.*

Follow the ritual with a water fight, swimming, a picnic, and other beach activities. If you do the ritual at home, play throwing games with balls or disks, or water games with squirt guns, sprinklers, or water balloons. Then have a picnic.

Lugnasad/Lammas

Lammas begins the harvest season. It's the feast of first fruits, the first of the three harvest festivals. Grain is ripening and the first apples are ready. Although the traditional date for Lammas and Lugnasad is August 1st, if you farm and have a major crop, celebrate the day (under the name "Feast of First Fruits") when that crop becomes ripe, and then again on the traditional date in honor of the grain. If your major crop is grain, celebrate the day once, when the grain starts to be ready to harvest.

Lammas derives its name from the Old English "Hlafmas," or "Loaf-mass." The name says it all: it's the feast of bread. The name is Christian, although the traditions it reflects are probably Pagan. On this day in early Christian times, loaves made from the first grain were blessed in the church. In Pagan times, they were almost certainly used in some ritual. Perhaps they were blessed and shared. Perhaps they were given as offerings to the gods. First-fruit offerings are nearly universal—the first of anything belongs to the gods. On this day, the first grain was cut in the morning and made into bread or porridge by evening. In Ireland, it was considered "just not done" to harvest grain before Lugnasad, because it was a sign that the previous year's harvest hadn't lasted long enough. This was taken as a serious failing, either on the part of the farmer for not growing enough, or on the part of his wife for not conserving the store.

The Gaelic word for this day, *Lugnasad* (also spelled *Lughnasadh*, and pronounced "Loo-nah-sah"), means "Assembly of Lug." Lug (whose name is also spelled "Lugh," and pronounced "Loo" in modern Irish) was a Celtic god who was worshipped across Europe. His name appears all over the place: the Roman name of the city of Carlisle, *Luguvalium*, means "Strong in Lug," and "Lyons" has its origin in his name as well. In Wales, he was *Lleu Llaw Gyffes* ("Lleu of the Skillful Hand"). In Ireland, he had the titles *Lug Samildánach* ("Lug Skilled in the Arts," pronounced "Loo Saw-vil-dah-nakh") and *Lug Lamhfada* ("Lug Long Arm," pronounced "Loo Lah-wah-duh"). *Lug* and *Lleu* may mean "bright" or "shining," which has led some to describe him as a solar god, but his myths connect him instead with other Indo-European storm gods, so his brightness is likely to be that of lightning.

Lug's titles go a long way toward describing him—he is the skillful one, the craftsman god. There is a wonderful story in the tale of *Cath Maige Tuired* (*The Battle of Mag Tuired*) of how Lug came to the court at Tara while a feast was going on. It was the custom there that no one was to be admitted during a feast unless they possessed a skill that no one who was already there possessed. Lug listed his skills one by one—wright, smith, champion, harper, hero, poet, magician, healer, cupbearer, craftsman—and the doorkeeper told him each time that there was already someone at Tara who possessed that skill. Finally, Lug asked if there was anyone who had *all* these skills. There was no one who did, and so he was allowed to enter.

This is the Lug we know from the tales—the god of skills and crafts, the shining ruler with the great spear (possibly of lightning). The date of his festival makes it possible that he was also an agricultural deity identified with the ripening of grain. This agricultural function is supported by the *Cath Maige Tuired*, where, after defeating Bres, Lug forced him to reveal the secrets of when to plough, sow, and reap.

There seem to be two themes for this date, then. One is the agricultural, taken from the Saxon Lammas traditions, and the other the honoring of work, skills, and crafts, taken from the Irish Lugnasad ones. I give two rituals here, then, one for Lammas and one for Lugnasad. Their common ground may be found in the blessing of agricultural tools before the harvest. Unless you're a grower of grain, that isn't going to be very relevant for you, though.

This day begins a strange time of the year. To most people, it's high summer. These are the hottest days of the year, a time for vacations and the beach. But look more closely. Crops are ripening. Pokeberries appear. And what is that about the light of late afternoon? Not only is it fading earlier each day, there is something in it that whispers "fall." Its angle is changing, and shadows are growing. No, it isn't time to turn toward the dark yet, not by any means. But we can feel the shadow behind us, hard on our heels. Soon the days will be cold and dark. That's why the bread at each of the harvest rituals grows progressively darker, as fall closes in.

For now, though, we can celebrate this strange time as a happy one—the Loaf Mass, the Feast of Lug. The sun is high; the days are long and hot. The wheat is golden, ready to be cut. And we reflect on the coming harvest, on all that we've accomplished. This is a time for sharing your bounty. Sometime during the harvest, between now and Samhain, give a major charitable donation. And leave out grain and bread for the wild animals in your area, even if these are just pigeons and sparrows.

Celebrating Lammas

Decorations: Sickles, scythes, garden vegetables, corn dollies, grain, grapes, vines, poppies, corn shocks.

Food: Early-harvest foods, especially those grown in your area. Grain products, corn on the cob, grapes, plums. Sometimes the early apples are available for Lammas. If so, be sure to include them.

Blessing the Harvest

Set the table with your best settings. Prepare all the food except that which will come from your own garden. This is the time for all harvests to be celebrated, so include anything you've produced since last Lammas—art, writing, crafts, music, money—any symbol of your work.

If you have a garden or farm, start the ritual there. In fact, if you have enough space and privacy, hold the entire ritual there or next to it, on a picnic table or even on the ground. If you don't grow any of your own food, include some grown in your local area. Many areas have farms where you can pick your own produce. Take your children to them so they see that food doesn't come from supermarkets.

Bake a loaf of white bread in the shape of a man. The simplest way to do this is to take the dough after it's finished its last rise and cut five slits in it (see Figure 8). Spread the top two sections out to form arms. Spread the two bottom pieces apart to form legs. Then round out the head part and bake. This bread will serve as the presence of the god whose seeds now stand in the field. Some of these seeds will be eaten, and some will be used to impregnate the earth again in the spring.

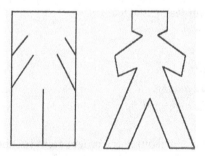

Figure 8. Harvest loaf baked in the shape of a man to symbolize the god whose seeds now stand growing in the fields.

When the table is set and the food ready, place the bread as a centerpiece and go out to your garden. The father or another adult holds a sickle. He hands it to one of those present, to harvest something, and then passes the sickle on. When all are done, and the sickle has gone full circle, the father says:

> *Harvest is beginning*
> *Gold Sun, bright days,*
> *Gold wheat, bright bread.*

He then uses the sickle to harvest something himself. If you don't have a garden, you can just say these words outdoors.

Then go in and gather around your table. The father lifts up the bread in his nondominant hand, holding the sickle in his dominant hand. He turns around slowly, presenting the bread and the sickle to the four directions, saying:

> *Harvest is beginning, now in the height of summer.*
> *Cold will have its turn but today it is warm.*
> *It is the feast of bright bread.*
> *It is the feast of first fruits.*
> *It is the hot time of the year*
> *while cold waits to creep in.*
> *Watch for the signs of fall:*
> *The fruits*
> *The berries*
> *The seeds*
> *They are coming.*
> *Soon the nights will be cold but now the days are hot.*

Then he holds the bread out to the other parent (or another adult), who holds their hands over it and says:

> *Our god is here, in the bread we eat.*

The father puts down the sickle and passes the bread around. Each person touches it in blessing and says:

> *We bless the bread,*
> *the bread blesses us.*

When the bread returns to the father, he blesses it and says:

> *We have all blessed the bread*
> *and now it will bless us.*

He cuts the head from the bread with the sickle and passes the bread around again, reserving the head. This time, everyone breaks off a piece of the bread. When everyone has a piece, all say (perhaps prompted by a parent):

> *The grain dies and we eat it and live.*
> *It blesses us and we thank it.*

Everyone eats a bit of the bread. Serve the rest with the dinner, and put any leftover bread out as an offering. You can use the head as an offering or bury it in the garden.

Blessing of the Tools

Before beginning this ritual, gather together your tools—laptop, toolbox, pencils, pots and pans, brooms—whatever you use in your work. If the item is too awkward, use a piece of the item or a symbol of it—a photograph or a power cord, for example.

Be sure to include your children's tools. School-age children can use their school supplies. If a child is starting school in the fall, this is a wonderful time to have their supplies ready so they can be blessed. Younger children can use their favorite toys. After all, the proper work of young children is play. Those old enough to have assigned chores can include the tools they use to perform them.

Put all the tools together on a table in the room where you eat, but not on the table you'll be eating on or there won't be room for the food. In the middle of the tools, put a candle with matches next to it. Wear the kind of clothes you wear when you work with these tools.

After the food is prepared and the table set with your best settings, stand around the table with the tools on it. Establish sacred time. An adult lights the candle, saying:

> *Be with us, Lug Samildánach,*
> *gifted in all the arts,*
> *possessor and giver of all skills.*
> *You who are open-handed, be here today to give us*
> > *your blessing.*

Each person then holds their hands over their own tools and says (either individually or together):

> *I bless these tools in Lug's name.*
> *I will use them well and properly in the service of the gods*
> > *and my people.*

Then have your meal and talk about what work you've done and what still remains to do.

Harvest

Fall is a uniquely ambivalent season. It's a happy time because of the harvest. It was traditionally a season when there was lots of food. Lots of work, but lots of food. Here in New England it's especially beautiful, and the air has a quality to it that defies description.

But fall is also a time of death. Those beautiful leaves are being stripped from the trees by the cold wind of the north and falling to the ground to rot. The plants in the fields have made their seeds and their work is done, so they grow brown and brittle. And the first hard frost runs its sickle through the tomatoes.

It's only fitting that there be this ambivalence, however. After all, fall includes the equinox, a time of balance, a crossover point when what came before and what's coming after are equally present. Harvest is one of the four solar festivals, and its message is that light and dark are in balance. Still, we know that although the dark may begin to prevail, Yule will come, and light return. From this knowledge, we gain the assurance to accept and even celebrate the wonderful death of the year.

The most important part of celebrating Harvest is feasting. Feasting, especially at harvest time, is a religious act. Eating large amounts of food in the company of family and friends is a way of thanking the earth, of cementing ties of love, and of reflecting the bounty of the season. You can celebrate Harvest as an early Thanksgiving (and there's no Pagan reason not to celebrate it on the secular day as well). Even if you do nothing else for this day, have a large festive meal. If preparation time is a problem, you can shift the celebration to a weekend, or take a day off from work and school.

For a meal to function as the centerpiece of a celebration, there must be special aspects to it, like particular foods eaten only on this holiday. These foods are usually time-consuming to make, very tasty, and not particularly good for you. Having a large number of people around the table is another desirable element, which is not only more festive but also allows you to practice hospitality. This is a time to invite friends and family, as many as you can handle, and as many as you think can handle helping you celebrate the day. On holidays, it's especially good luck to extend hospitality to a stranger, or perhaps to a friend of a friend.

Make sure to include whole-wheat bread baked in the shape of a sun in the meal. Any whole-wheat recipe will do. You can add sunflower seeds to it if you like. To shape the bread, divide the dough in two after its final rising, with one piece roughly three times the size of the other. Shape the smaller piece into a round loaf. Roll the larger piece into a long cylinder, then flatten it slightly and cut it into triangles. Although six is a traditional solar number, I suggest making more triangles than that or your sun will look like a turtle. (Trust me on this one.) Attach the triangles to the round loaf to form the sun's rays, using an egg-and-water mixture to stick them on. Then bake the bread according to the recipe you are using. Another way to avoid making a whole-wheat turtle is to shape the bread into a circle and cut a sun into it immediately before putting it in the oven.

The first ritual given below is a celebration that may appeal more to those who don't want thoughts of death to intrude too strongly into this time of year. The second puts a stronger emphasis on the dying of the year. Both rituals are written to be done indoors. If it's warm and you have a farm or a large garden, do them there. Both are rituals for which you may want to dress down, wearing the clothes you wear when you work in your garden, for instance.

Celebrating the Harvest

Decorations: Sunflower seeds, and seeds in general. They can be glued on paper or cardboard to make collages. Sickles, scythes, suns, and autumn leaves. Fall decorations in general.

Foods and drink: Seeds and foods made from seeds, foods that keep for the winter (roots and squashes), apples, goose, cider.

Farewell to the Light

At one end of your table, put something harvested from your garden and a bunch of dried ears of corn. Put your sun candle in the center and place the sun bread next to it. When all the food is ready and the table set with your best dishes, establish sacred time. Then an adult says:

> Today the wheel has come to a special point.
> For half the year now there has been more light than dark.
> Since Midsummer though, the light has been fading
> and today dark and light are equal
> Tomorrow the dark half of the year will begin.
> That is why we celebrate today.
> It is the balance point between light and dark.
> It is the beginning of the return of cold and dark.
> To the light time as it leaves we say Hail and farewell!

All repeat:

> Hail and farewell!

Light the sun candle and then continue:

> *To the dark time as it comes in we say Welcome!*
> *Be gentle with your cold, be loving in your dark.*
> *To the light time as it leaves we say Hail and farewell!*

All repeat:

> *Hail and farewell!*

Hold up the bread and the corn, and say:

> *All summer, the food has been growing and now Harvest is here.*
> *These are both sacred grains—*
> *corn, the sacred grain of this country,*
> *wheat, the sacred grain of our ancestors.*
> *We bless them.*
> *May they bless us.*

All repeat the last two lines.

Pass the bread around, with each person taking a piece and eating it. Then eat your meal. Afterward, hang the corn on your front door, saying:

> *Hang here till Samhain comes and the world grows*
> *   darker still.*
> *Hang here and bless our house*
> *and all our coming in and all our going out.*

You may want to leave the corn there at least until Thanksgiving, the traditional Harvest celebration in American culture. In fact, you can celebrate the first, solar, part of the ritual on the equinox and the second, harvest, part on Thanksgiving.

Save part of the bread for offerings to your household guardians and also for the spirits of the wild.

Welcoming Winter's Cold and Dark

Set the table with your best dishes, your sun candle, the sun bread, some matches, some dried leaves, and a pot. Leave a door to the outside at least partway open. When the food is ready to serve and everyone is at the table, establish sacred time. Then an adult goes to the door, slams it, and says:

> *Outdoor time is over and indoor time begins.*
> *More and more, now, we will be pulling ourselves in.*

Another adult lights the sun candle, saying:

> *He is in our midst, the lord of the sky.*

That person then picks up the dried leaves, lights them from the candle, and burns them in the pot, saying:

> *The Sun leaps up, the Sun dies down.*
> *It fades, it passes, and darkness comes*
> *but with one last flash of light.*

This may make a lot of smoke. If this bothers you, do it outside at the beginning of the ritual and then come inside, slamming the door on the way in. You may also want to disconnect the smoke alarm for the duration of this ritual. Don't forget to reconnect it after you're done, though. Then use the ashes to put a mark on the faces and hands of everyone present, saying:

> *In a flash of fire, the autumn leaves burn*
> *and leave behind the ashes of winter.*

Leave these marks on until the end of the meal, then wipe them off with a wet cloth. The one doing the wiping says:

> *The rains of spring will come again and bring life from*
> *the ashes.*

After the meal, at the end of either ritual, blow out the sun candle, saying:

The sun has gone into the fruits of summer and now it fades from the sky.

Celebrating Deities

In addition to calendar-based celebrations, you may also want to celebrate days dedicated to deities you're especially devoted to. We know about some of these rituals from ancient traditions, especially in Rome, where certain days of each month were dedicated to particular deities. For instance, the Kalends (the first day of the moon) was dedicated to Juno, while the Ides (the Full Moon) was dedicated to Jupiter. In addition, entire months were dedicated to certain deities—April to Venus, for instance. Rituals were also performed to commemorate the founding days of temples, which then provided dates for celebrating the deities to whom the temples were dedicated (see Scullard).

Other traditions, especially the Celtic and Germanic, give us less information. One exception to this is a holy day dedicated to Epona (December 18th), which appears on a calendar from Lombardy. This is often described as a Roman calendar (which it technically is), but the day is recorded only once and Lombardy was a Celtic region, so the information is less than definitive. It might be appropriate to honor other deities connected with horses then, though, such as Rhiannon, Macha, or Medb.

Egyptian Pagans might want to celebrate the "epagomenal days"—the five days (six in a Leap Year) that were added to bring the lunar year into line with the solar one. Originally starting with the helical rising of Sirius, they were fixed to August 24th through August 28th in the time of Augustus. Each day was dedicated to a different deity—first Osiris, then Horus, then Set, then Isis, and finally Nepthys. The month following these days was named after Thoth, and some other days throughout the year were dedicated to deities as well. Each of these deities could receive special honor on their day through a more elaborate version of the daily ritual described in chapter 3.

You may have trouble finding information on days dedicated to particular deities in some traditions. There are ways to help overcome this, however. Some deities are associated with one of the holidays I've already talked about—Lug's association with Lugnasad is an obvious example, as is Brigid's connection to Brigid's Day (Imbolc). Freyr is connected with Yule. These deities, and others connected with them, can be honored at those times. I recommend, though, that you either honor the deity on a day near the seasonal holiday but not actually on it, or the other way round. Holiday celebrations can be labor- and time-intensive, so trying to celebrate both on the same day can be tiring and take all the fun out of the rituals. And trying to do two celebrations at once can tend to take away from the importance of one or both, with the holiday in particular overwhelming the honoring of the deity.

Another way is to look at what deities from other traditions may be connected with your own deity. You can then honor your deity on a day connected with the other tradition. It's fashionable to say that, since the Romans were enemies of the Celts and even conquered most of the Celtic lands, the deities of those two traditions shouldn't be associated with one another. The ancient Pagans would have strongly disagreed with this, however. We see inscriptions to deities that combine Celtic and Roman names—for instance, Lenus Mars from Trier—and we see other cases in which statues and reliefs combine gods from both traditions. The relief of Smertrios on the Pillar of the Sailors in Paris, for instance, is almost identical to pillars depicting Hercules.

Another way to choose a date for these celebrations is through divination. For this, you can use whatever method you're used to, or one that's connected with the tradition you're exploring. Runes would be good for a Germanic deity, for instance.

Finally, there's something called UPG—Unverified Personal Gnosis. UPG happens when you sense that something is right according to your own ideas. These insights can come from conclusions drawn from lore, or just from your own intuition. Lug can be connected via UPG with employment, work, or project management, for instance, since he assigned jobs to the various Irish deities in the *Cath Maige Tuired*. (I'm grateful to Nevin Flanagan for this suggestion.) Thus a day on which you started a career might be a good one to honor him on. Likewise, a deity associated with learning, like Thoth, might properly receive worship on the day you received a degree. And so on.

A traditional Indo-European way to honor deities is to call them, offer to them, share a meal with them, and then say goodbye. Here's a ritual for doing this in your home. Even though only one member of a family may be dedicated to a particular deity, that deity's protection is a concern to everyone in the household, so all family members should take part in the ritual. The person whose deity is being honored will take the major role, of course, but some parts can be assigned to others, like making offerings.

Before beginning the ritual, put a bowl and a plate on the table in front of the place where the image and fire will later be placed (preferably in the east). Also put a piece of bread there on another plate, along with a bottle or pitcher containing an offering appropriate to the deity.

Begin by having everyone purify themselves, and then establish sacred time. If you have an image of the deity, you can purify that as well. If you want, you can reinforce the sacred cosmos in a way similar to the one you used when you consecrated your shrine. At least light the fire. Follow this with a prayer to the deity. A traditional form of Pagan prayer is to mention the deity by name or title, then say something about what they've done in the past, either mythically or in your own life. Remind the deity of things you've done for *them* in the past as well, make an offering, and then make any request you might have. These elements can be broken up into sections of a larger ritual, which is what I do here. I'll give a ritual for Zeus. but it can easily be adapted for other deities.

Calling and Honoring Zeus

The person whose deity is being honored (or a parent if that's not possible) lights the fire in the household shrine and says:

> Zeus, King of the Gods,
> You who uphold the Law,
> who protect guests and inspire all to respect the rules of
>   hospitality,
> defeater of the Titans who opposed the Olympians,
> and of all who seek to overthrow divine Order,
> I pray to you.
> I ask you to remember the offerings I have given you
>   in the past
> and come to those who worship you today.

The person who's dedicated to the deity then carries the deity's image to the table, while someone else carries the fire. If there's no image of the deity present, the child (or parent) can carry the fire. Either way, when the image and fire are both put down, the child (or parent) says:

> We have established you in our home.

The child (or parent) pours an offering into the bowl, saying:

> Father Zeus, God of Hospitality:
> with this offering we welcome you to our meal,
> we share with you our riches.

They child (or parent) then puts the piece of bread on the offering plate, saying:

> Father Zeus, who looks down on the Earth from your place
>   in the heavens:
> we offer you food from the Earth;
> we share with you our riches.

The offerings you make may vary with the deity, as will the prayers.

Then eat a good meal, using your best dishes. You may want to give the deity bits of each kind of food you eat at the meal, although this isn't necessary. I think it would be nice to give them some of your dessert, though, since that's the sweetest part of the meal.

After the meal, take the deity's image and the fire back to the shrine and put them in their normal place, saying:

> *Zeus, Ruler of Gods and Men,*
> *even though we say goodbye to you now,*
> *be present when you are needed,*
> *to watch over and give that for which you are well-known,*
> *to me, to all those I love, and to this home*
> *and to all who enter it as guests.*
> *Goodbye for now then.*

Extinguish the fire, end sacred time, and you're done.

CHAPTER 9

Betrothals, Weddings, Partings

When children grow up, they leave home. Some leave to set up households of their own. Some move in with friends. And some get married. Yes, they do—as hard as that may be to believe when your children are small.

Parents are in a delicate position when it comes to weddings. Some try to take over their child's wedding completely. The unfortunate ones succeed. But, just as each member of a married couple is a blend of family traditions and unique qualities, about to be joined with another such blend, so too should their wedding be a blend. It's *their* wedding, mothers and fathers, and although you may get your say, they get the last word. If you trust them enough to make the decision to be married, surely you can trust them with the getting married part.

My advice up to this point has been directed at telling adults what can be done with children. Adults, this is my advice: turn the wedding over to the children. I am turning this chapter over to them.

Okay, kids (and you better not be kids if you are getting married), forget what I just said. You're not in this alone. Weddings are family affairs, make no mistake about that. Family members of all generations come together at weddings, not only to watch, but to participate.

Their very presence is an affirmation of both the joining of two lives and of marriage in general. And because this gathering of generations almost guarantees the presence of non-Pagans at the event, weddings are a good time to introduce non-Pagan relatives to your ways. A beautiful wedding can draw in even the most stubborn objectors.

Remember this as you plan the wedding, and remember that little things may make all the difference in the world. Talk to people who will be guests and whose opinion you value. Listen for key phrases like: "It just isn't a wedding without . . ." or "I love it at weddings when . . . ." It may turn out that all it takes to placate Great-Aunt Mildred is the right kind of cake. The very fact that you ask their opinions may be enough to make people feel valued and thereby have good feelings toward both the wedding and the marriage. A good marriage is a compromise. The wedding is a good place to start.

I'm not saying that you should compromise your religious values, of course. You have every right to be married in a Pagan way. But please keep in mind that a wedding belongs in part to the community and that the members of that community should have their say as well. If you want non-Pagan people to be there, surely you want their approval as well.

Betrothals

It's customary in many cultures for a wedding to consist of two parts—the betrothal and the wedding ceremony. The period between these two events may last for days or for years. The traditional length of a Wiccan betrothal is a year and a day, although the time may vary according to a couple's needs. In our culture, betrothals are replaced by engagements, which mark a serious step with certain privileges and responsibilities. While engagements can be broken, that usually only happens with some difficulty.

An early form of betrothal was a Gaelic custom called "handfasting." Handfasting was seen as a trial marriage that lasted for a year and a day, at the end of which it was dissolved or made permanent. The name of this Gaelic tradition has become the Neo-Pagan term for a wedding, and a very pretty word it is too. While the term "handfasting" may now refer to weddings, it should still be remembered that the original tradition was one of betrothal.

The customs used by popular culture to mark the betrothed status—tokens like engagement rings—are in keeping with Pagan tradition, although it's best when these gifts are mutual. The exchange of such tokens is a part of betrothal traditions everywhere. Indeed, in the Indo-European tradition, it's by the exchange of gifts that all relationships are established. In some places, the traditional gift is an item of some sort that's broken, with each party keeping half. Popular tokens include coins, belts, and bracelets. The symbolism of binding, enclosing, and the infinity of the circle is common to many of these items.

Betrothal Ceremony

The decision to marry is, of course, a private one, made at a private moment. After the decision is made, though, the couple should gather both families together to announce it. Tokens may be exchanged at this time, and toasts made. These acts are usually sealed with a kiss. Before the toasts, the parents of the couple tie the couple's hands together with a natural fiber cord, saying:

> Now you are bound, one to the other,
> with a tie not easy to break.
> Take this time of binding before the final vows are made
> to learn what you need to know
> to grow in wisdom and love
> that your marriage might be strong
> that your love might last.

After the toasts, the cord can be removed by the parents and given to the couple to be kept safe.

At betrothal ceremonies, offerings should be made to the family guardians of both families. Their images can be brought to the announcement ritual, or the couple can present themselves the next time they visit their parents' homes, officially introducing the new family member (even if they've met before). If it's impossible to gather both families, the announcement can made in front of other witnesses.

Weddings

A wedding isn't just an agreement between two people. It's a ritual that's effective on three planes: the individual, the social, and the cosmic. That marriage affects the individual plane is obvious. That it affects the social plane will be made painfully clear by the families of the couple taking vows. Have patience with them; a wedding is an important step in the continuation of the community.

But it's on the cosmic plane that Pagan weddings come into their own. A bride and a groom stand at the moment of creation. Through them, the world is renewed. They are queen and king, priestess and priest, goddess and god. In ancient Greece, weddings imitated the wedding of Zeus and Hera. In Hindu weddings, the groom says to his bride: "I am heaven, you are earth." And in the ritual which will be given here, the bride and groom are consecrated as divinities and paid homage.

Since a wedding is a new beginning, elements of wedding rituals are frequently shared with New Years' rituals and vice versa. In ancient Sumer, for instance, the ritual for the new year climaxed with a reenactment of the creation story, which included a marriage between the king and the Goddess, between earth and heaven. This is the sort of thing a bride and groom are getting themselves into.

The ceremony below requires a priest and a priestess. In many places, it's possible to find Pagan priests and priestesses who are legally qualified to perform wedding ceremonies. It's also often possible for anyone to obtain a one-day license to perform a marriage. Check your local laws to see if this is possible. If this isn't true where you live and you want to have someone who's not licensed officiate, a civil wedding can be performed either before or after the religious one, with only the minimum number of people attending. This will prevent the civil ceremony from being seen as the "real" wedding.

Couples often approach their wedding with a combination of joy and fear. It's only right that they should; a wedding is a cusp, an initiation, a moment when a couple's lives will be changed forever. This proper state shouldn't be too hard to achieve; it is, after all, the natural state of couples getting married.

Couples should spend the night before their wedding separately, even if they already live together. In creating a marriage, they are coming together, not just from their aloneness, but from their birth families. It's nice, then, if they can spend the last night of their unmarried lives with those families. This isn't just good ritual symbolism; it may make their parents very happy. The couple should spend at least some time, either the night before or in the morning of the wedding, in meditation and/ or prayer, alone or with a few friends, to prepare themselves spiritually. When they get up on the day of the wedding, they should perform whatever purification ritual is used in their tradition.

If the betrothed couple don't have a traditional purification ritual, they can start with a bath with cleansing herbs in the water (yarrow and hawthorn are traditional wedding herbs) and then meditate for a while, which will also help them calm themselves. They should call upon their gods and goddesses to bless the wedding and the marriage. If they still live at home or are leaving for the wedding from home, they must pray to the family guardians, asking for peace between the guardians and themselves as they move out and establish their own family. The guardians should be given a final offering, perhaps incense and hair, before each of the couple leaves their family homes.

Because weddings mark the beginning of a new life, couples should fast, consuming only milk, the food of babies. This Roman custom also introduces one of the themes of this ritual. Dionysos is usually thought of as a god of wine, and indeed he is. But he is also a god of faithful marriage. After Theseus had abandoned Ariadne, Dionysos found her. They were married, and he was faithful to her, not a common state of things among the Graeco-Roman deities. Since Dionysos is also the god of liquids, especially those that flow through and from living things, he's called upon in this wedding ritual by using three drinks: milk, water, and wine.

Wedding dates are often a matter of convenience. If possible, however, the date should be significant. Lugnasad (August 1st) is the traditional date for weddings in Scotland. In Ireland, weddings were traditionally held on the date that marked the end of the year and a day of betrothal. At Tailteann, a fair was held on Lugnasad where marriages were arranged that could then be dissolved at the next fair. This is the date of my own anniversary, of a marriage that has fortunately remained strong. One advantage of this date for me is that it makes my anniversary impossible to forget. (I've got a bad memory.)

May Day and Midsummer are also good times for weddings. In some Neo-Pagan traditions, one or the other of these days is celebrated as the wedding day of the Goddess and the God. The Romans considered May to be an unlucky month for weddings, giving rise to the tradition of June weddings. In Paganism as it's practiced today, though, May Day is perfectly suitable. It should be noted, however, that, in Celtic tradition, May Day is a day for very impermanent matings, for one-night stands. So if you practice in a Celtic tradition, that may not be a good day for your wedding. If none of these dates is practical, make an effort to schedule the wedding for the waxing of the moon, especially the day the new moon is first visible. As the moon grows, so might the marriage.

Dress for weddings is a personal choice. Some Pagans wear ritual garb, while others choose traditional American clothes. White dresses aren't inappropriate for Pagan weddings, because, contrary to popular opinion, the wearing of white has nothing to do with virginity, but rather is only limited to first weddings. This makes sense, since white is a traditional color for initiations and new beginnings.

There's no Pagan reason to refrain from most of the customs that surround weddings in our culture. It's true, of course, that some of these traditions may have meanings a Pagan will find offensive. If something offends you, don't do it. But if you really want to do something but wonder what other Pagans will think, you're missing the whole point of tradition. Many traditions are done simply because they're what's usually done in a particular situation. "This is what my parents did" is a perfectly Pagan sentiment. Does anybody really think of the meaning of being carried over the threshold while it's being done? If you find meaning in something (and simply being fun is meaning enough), then go ahead and do it. Reinterpret it if necessary, but do it.

Many wedding traditions of the various ethnic groups in our country are also appropriate at a Pagan wedding (and may go far toward making peace with a family upset about having a Pagan ceremony). Throwing grain, a wedding cake, traditional dances—there's nothing inherently un-Pagan about these. In fact, some of them are of Pagan origin.

Weather permitting, Pagan weddings should be held outside, in contact with the earth and under the gaze of the sky. If this isn't possible, the couple should go outside at some point after the ceremony to call on earth and sky as witnesses.

Pagan Wedding Ceremony

Few Pagans have the luxury of a temple or other sacred space large enough to hold a wedding of any size, and weddings rarely take place in the home these days. It will therefore usually be necessary to consecrate the area where the ceremony will take place. If you are Wiccan, this means casting a circle. If you belong to some other tradition, form sacred space according to your usual practice. For instance, if you work in a Celtic or Germanic tradition, you can establish sacred space in the same way that you used when you established your home shrine. Just use a larger well, fire, and tree, to fit the scale of the space, and set them perpendicular to the seats of the guests so everyone can see all three. Perform the major part of the ritual with the fire between the guests and the couple, to emphasize the couple's sacred nature, as if they're coming to the fire as deities. The instructions given here are for a Wiccan circle that's specifically appropriate for a wedding. This circle isn't intended to keep power in or spirits out. Instead, it defines an area that's been blessed and declared sacred. The spirits of the four directions are called and reverenced, but no wall is established between the sacred and profane worlds.

In the place where the ritual will be performed, form a circle from flowers to mark the edge of the sacred space. Guests can stand or sit outside or inside the flower circle, depending on how many guests and flowers you have. Make sure you provide chairs for those who need them and for any guests who are dressed in traditional American wedding clothes, which aren't well suited for sitting on the ground. If the day's hot, there should definitely be seats, and an awning for shade may be necessary as well. The bulk of the guests should be sitting or standing in the south or west to allow room in the north or east, depending on the direction your tradition's rituals are usually oriented towards. The ritual below is oriented toward the north. As the canonical Indo-European direction for prayers, east is particularly appropriate for Celtic or Germanic weddings.

Put a table in the center of the circle to serve as an altar. It can be any table of a convenient height that's large enough to hold a wand, incense (with charcoal if necessary), two white candles, a third candle (white, yellow, or red), a bowl of water, a symbol of earth (salt, sand, a good-sized rock, or a crystal), matches, three cups (two may be matching and one different, preferably taller than the others), a pitcher of water, a pitcher or bottle of wine, a crown of ivy or grain for one partner (traditionally the groom), and a crown of flowers for the other (traditionally the bride). If the ceremony's held outside, all the candles should be in jars to keep them from being blown out. The rings may also be on the table, traditionally on the wand, or the best man and maid of honor may carry them. Lean a broom—preferably the old-fashioned round kind—against the table.

Put a torch or a white candle in a jar on tall stands or small tables at each of the four directions. You can decorate the poles of the torches or the stands or tables with ribbons and/or flowers. If you put a lighter by each candle, it will make lighting them go more smoothly. Alternatively, those who light the candles can carry the lighters.

At a Wiccan ceremony, a priest and priestess are required to ensure the blessing of both the God and Goddess. When everything is ready, these officiants enter and stand behind the altar, and then welcome everyone. This is also the time to explain to the guests what will happen.

There will usually be non-Pagans present who will need to be put at ease. A printed program giving the text or at least an outline of the ritual will help. If the program gives enough detail, it may be possible to eliminate the spoken explanation entirely, improving the flow of the ritual, but a welcome is still polite.

Have the people who are to serve as the representatives of the guardians of the elements go to their appropriate directions and stand on the outside of the tables there. Since Water and Earth are traditionally thought of as female, and Air and Fire as male, the representatives can be of the corresponding sex, although this is best left up to the couple. In the calling of the elements given here, the priest calls the male elements and the priestess calls the female ones, but this is flexible as well. The elemental representatives may be part of the procession, in which case they will be with the wedding couple at this point. If that's the case, they'll be responsible for invoking the elements into themselves before the procession.

After the welcome, the priestess lights the two white candles on the altar table to signify that sacred time has begun. You can also have someone sound a bell, a gong, or a drum. The priestess then goes about the space with the wand, saying:

> *Blessed be this circle,*
> *a meeting place for the gods and their people,*
> *a meeting place of love.*

If the priestess doesn't generally use a wand, her hand will serve, although a wand is more striking at a public ritual like this.

The priest then lights the incense and brings it once around the circle, starting and ending in the east. In the east, he holds it up and says:

> *Power of the East*
> *Power of Air*
> *Be with us here in this sacred place*
> *to bless the two who will come before you.*

The priest waves the incense over the representative of Air and puts it on the table. The representative then lights the candle on the table. (If the representatives of the elements are going to come in with the wedding couple, the priest or priestess will need to light the candles.) The priest then goes to the altar and lights the white, yellow, or red candle, then brings it once around the circle, starting and ending in the south. He holds the candle up and says:

> *Powers of the South*
> *Powers of Fire*
> *be with us here in this sacred place*
> *to bless the two who will come before you.*

He moves the candle in a circle around the head of the representative of Fire and then puts it on the table. The representative (or the priest) then lights the candle, and the priest goes to the altar, where he stands facing the guests.

The priestess then picks up the bowl of water from the altar and brings it once around the circle, starting and ending in the west. She holds it up and says:

> *Powers of the West,*
> *Powers of Water,*
> *be with us here in this sacred place*
> *to bless the two who will come before you.*

She sprinkles some on the representative of Water and puts it on the table. The representative (or the priestess) lights the candle. The priestess then goes to the altar and picks up the symbol of Earth. She brings it once around the circle, starting and ending in the north, then holds the symbol up and says:

> *Powers of the North*
> *Powers of Earth*
> *be with us here in this sacred place*
> *to bless the two who will come before you.*

She holds the symbol against the forehead of the representative of Earth (if it is salt or sand, she may sprinkle some of it on them) and puts it on the table. The representative (or the priestess) lights the candle. Then the priestess returns to the altar and stands on its north side, to the left of the priest. The priest stretches out his hands, palms up, and says:

> Lady of Love,
> We ask your presence here
> to bless the two who will come before you.

He drops his hands and the priestess raises hers and says:

> Lord of Love,
> We ask your presence here
> to bless the two who will come before you.

She then drops her hands. If the couple prefer particular Goddess and God names, they can use them instead of "Lady of Love" and "Lord of Love."

During the establishing of sacred space, the bride and groom will have been elsewhere. After the casting, someone previously chosen by them leaves the circle and goes to get them. Alternatively, a drum, a gong, a bell, or a horn may be sounded to call them.

The couple's entrance can be as elaborate a processional as they wish. They may be preceded by someone with a torch or flowers, with the main cup for the ritual, or with ringing bells. They may come in to music, accompanied by attendants (ushers, bridesmaids, a flower girl, parents, etc.). Wedding attendants are an almost universal custom, and it's only natural to want friends with you on a journey of this sort. On the other hand, the couple may prefer to come in alone. The only requirement for this entrance is that they not be touching each other. This is because of the ritual and psychological principle that deliberate abstention from something increases its effectiveness when it's finally achieved. The couple is not joined together yet.

If the couple enters with their parents, they should say goodbye to them at the edge of the circle. The parents then go to where they'll sit for the rest of the ceremony, and the couple turns to face the priest and priestess, who go to the edge of the circle, facing the couple. From inside the circle, the priest and priestess challenge the couple, saying, either together or in turn:

> *Who comes before us?*

Each answers by name. They are challenged again:

> *Why do you come before us today?*

Each answers:

> *I wish to become one with [name].*

They are challenged again:

> *What do you offer to each other as token?*

They answer:

> *Perfect love and perfect trust.*

The priest and priestess then say:

> *All who bring such are doubly welcome.*

(These challenges are based on the first-degree initiation ritual of Gardnerian Wicca.)

After the challenges, the couple is brought into the circle and greeted with kisses from the priest and priestess. They are then brought to each quarter in turn. At the east, the representative of Air says:

> *The blessing of Air be upon this couple.*
> *Air is the quick change, hard to catch,*

> The wind that blows through life.
> Throw yourself onto it, and let it bear you up.

The representative then moves the incense or waves it with a paper fan or feather so that the smoke touches the couple. At the south, the representative of Fire says:

> The blessing of Fire be upon this couple.
> Fire burns away all that is impure.
> It is the passion that drew you together
> and the hearth flame that will keep your home happy.

The representative brings the candle close enough to the couple so they can feel its heat and then returns it to the table. At the west, the representative of Water says:

> The blessing of Water be upon this couple.
> Water is the womb, the essence of life.
> It is the slow change, gracefully dancing.
> Rest in its flow, and let it hold you up.

The representative sprinkles the couple with the water. At the north, the representative of Earth says:

> The blessing of Earth be upon this couple.
> Earth is stability, solidity, existence.
> It is cold and dark and empty.
> But out of darkness, comes light
> Out of cold, comes life
> Out of the empty days, comes love
> And out of these three, comes happiness.

The representative touches the symbol of Earth to the foreheads of the couple.

The couple are then brought to the north, where they stand facing away from each other, with one on the west and one on the east. (If the couple is a man and a woman, the man traditionally stands on the east and the woman on the west.) The priest and priestess each pour wine into one of the two matching cups, then the priest goes to stand in front of one member of the couple and the priestess in front of the other. They offer the cup of wine to their corresponding member, saying:

> *Wine is ecstasy, a path of magic,*
> *the way to the Gods, a sign of life.*

After drinking, the couple kneel. The priest and priestess bless them, stretching their arms over them while speaking. The priestess says:

> *Gentle Goddess, attest the union of these young hearts.*

The priest says:

> *Mighty God, attest the union of these young hearts.*

The priestess says:

> *Ever-Changing Moon, attest the union of these young hearts.*

The priest says:

> *Unconquered Sun, attest the union of these young hearts.*

The priestess says:

> *Land and Sea, attest the union of these young hearts.*

The priest says:

> *Air and Void, attest the union of these young hearts.*

The priestess says:

> *May all who are witnesses here*

The priest says:

and all who may encounter them

Together they say:

attest the union of these young hearts.

(The words "attest the union of these young hearts," are a slightly modified quotation from the Alexandrian *Book of Shadows* and can be repeated by the guests with its last utterance.)

The priest or priestess then uses the broom to sweep away all impurities and bad luck from the couple, and then place it on the ground behind them. The priest crowns one partner (traditionally the bride), saying:

You are she, the One without Beginning.
You are the Mother of All, who gives birth to the world.
You are the Essence from whom all things are formed.
Wherever we may look, you will be there.
You are She of Many Names:
When your true face is known, all naming ceases.
In your presence, all stop to wonder.
All life is a prayer to you.

The priestess then crowns the other partner (traditionally the groom), saying:

You are he who dies and rises again and again.
You are the Father of All, born in every moment.
You are Existence, the form shown by all things.
Wherever we may look, you will be there.
You are He of Many Names.
Though we lift your mask, there is no end to the naming.
In your presence, all stop to wonder.
All life is a prayer to you.

(If the couple is of the same sex, the same prayer can be used for both of them.)

The priest and priestess then give the couple the rings (or the rings may be given them by an attendant). They turn to face each other, take each other's hands, and say in turn:

> *I take you to my hand*
> *at the rising of the moon,*
> *at the setting of the stars,*
> *to love and to honor*
> *through all that may come,*
> *through all our life together.*

As they say these words, they put the rings on each other's hands. If they wish to make a further commitment, they may say:

> *In all our lives,*
> *may we be reborn in the same time and at the same place*
> *that we may meet, and know, and remember, and love again.*

The first three lines of the first prayer and the last two lines of the second are from the Gardnerian *Book of Shadows*.

One partner then pours water into the remaining cup and offers it to the other. After drinking, this partner pours in more water and offers it back to the other, who drinks.

This is the third drink in the ceremony. First came milk, the food of babies, drunk by the couple in separate places. Then came wine, food of gods, which was drunk as adults in each other's presence, but from separate cups. Now the couple have transcended their individuality and bonded to each other by drinking water—pure liquidity—from the same cup. Thus the liquids have been drunk in such a way that the couple has come closer and closer together until, after their final joining through vows, rings, and water, they are one.

The cup used in the wedding is an emblem of the couple's life together, and so it must be new. After the wedding, the couple will keep the cup, perhaps to be passed around at family rituals, used to drink toasts to the ancestors, or kept for other special occasions. If, may the gods forbid, the marriage should end in divorce, it will be needed for the ritual of parting (see below). For this reason, it should be breakable, but more so to convey the message that the marriage which has been created through it must be guarded if it's to remain whole.

After putting the water and cup back on the altar, the couple kiss, turn, and jump over the broom. This is a Romany custom that probably originated in Germany and the Netherlands and has now made its way into Neo-Paganism. Then the music starts, the couple recess, and the guests leave to go to the reception.

Between the ceremony and the reception, the new couple should spend some time alone together. During this time, a bride may wish to follow an old custom and put her hair up. This would continue a custom that is based on the connection between marital status and hairstyle found among many peoples, among them the Romans and the Slavs. In these traditions, a female partner marks the transition from maiden to matron, with all its attendant responsibilities, by putting up her hair.

One of the most practiced wedding customs in modern America involves carrying over the threshold. This tradition comes from the Romans. Since a Roman wife moved into her husband's house, her entry was an important event. To stumble on the threshold would be an insult to the gods of her new household, so this possibility was prevented by carrying her over it. Even if this custom is objected to as patrilocal, the threshold guardians of the couple's new home still have to be honored. Entering into a house after marriage to set up a new household is a sacred act. This, then, is a good time to perform a house blessing ritual (see chapter 3). Even if the couple has lived together before marriage, their wedding establishes a new household, and this must be recognized ritually.

The establishment of a new household requires the acquisition of new family guardians. (The ritual for this is given in chapter 3.) Articles for the shrine, like candles and offering bowls, are thus a good choice for wedding presents from the parents of the couple. It would be especially appropriate for the parents of a bride to give a statue of a female guardian and a groom's family to give a statue of a male guardian. If the couple prefer to make their own guardian images, they can be given the materials to do that instead.

The traditional year-and-a-day requirement for betrothals can be met in two ways. Of course, an engagement can simply last that long, with the wedding acting as a confirming event. Alternatively, the wedding can be considered the beginning of the period. In this case, the ceremony of tying the hands can take place at the wedding after the rings are exchanged, and before the sharing of water with the priest or priestess, dropping the part starting with "take this time of binding."

If the period of a year and a day starts at the wedding, the end of that period should be observed with a ritual and a party, attended at least by the priest, the priestess, and the two legal witnesses from the wedding. This ritual can be a simple declaration by the couple that the marriage will continue—and then on to the party.

Partings

Divorce should never be easy and, people being what they are, it rarely is. And since a marriage begins with a ritual, it's suitable that it should end with one as well. A divorce is as sacred an act as a wedding, and a ceremony to mark this act may help ease some of the pain, while at the same time validating the parting. Such rituals have been lacking in most religious communities, but Pagans have been making an effort to develop them.

Just as weddings aren't solely a personal act, neither are partings. If a couple has children, this is obvious, and every effort must be made to minimize problems the breakup of the marriage may cause them. Our Mother and Father expect no less.

It's not so obvious, perhaps, that a divorce affects the community. So if the community is called upon to witness a wedding, it should also be called upon to witness a parting. This is not to suggest that you should throw a large party, complete with a sit-down dinner and dancing. But there are people who were important in the creation of the marriage who deserve to be a part in its dissolution. Of course, divorces aren't always friendly, so this ritual may not always be possible. But if a couple is Pagan, they owe it to themselves and to their community to make the effort. Through it, some healing may come to all. At least it can begin.

Perform the ritual below only after the legal process of divorce is final. The ritual should be the last act in the divorce, marking its completion. If possible, gather together the priest and priestess who presided at the wedding, as well as the two witnesses that are required by law in most places. These witnesses stand in for the community. If the two witnesses who attended the wedding can't be present, choose two people who are acceptable to both members of the couple, or one who's acceptable to each partner.

Because this ritual involves planting seeds, it's best done outdoors. Even in a city, you can probably find some appropriate spot—a secluded corner of a park, a vacant lot, even a roadside if necessary. Since the place may acquire painful associations as a result of the ritual, try to choose a place that the couple won't pass by or encounter regularly. If the ceremony absolutely can't be performed outdoors, choose a location that's neutral. Strong feelings may well be released during the ritual, so the location needs to be one where both members of the couple feel at home, or at least a place where they feel equally *not* at home.

Pagan Parting Ceremony

Place a cord of natural fibers on a small table. If possible, use the cord that joined the couple in the betrothal or wedding. For an inside ritual, you can use thread or string instead of rope. You will also need a knife, a cup filled with water, and some seeds. If at all possible, use the cup the couple drank from at their wedding. Whatever cup you use, it must be breakable. You'll also need two rocks or hammers with which to break the cup, and a natural-fiber bag to put it in so it can be broken safely.

Prepare a small hole in the ground, leaving the spade you dig with next to it. If the ceremony is being performed indoors, you'll need a large paper bag half-filled with dirt and some additional dirt to fill it the rest of the way. If you wish to call sacred space according to your tradition, do so here. Once you are ready, the couple, the husband and wife, say to the others:

> *You who stood with us at the beginning of this marriage:*
> *We have asked you to be here at its end*
> *that you might see that it is done rightly.*

The couple may want to alternate with the first two lines and then say the last line together.

Have the priest or priestess tie the couple's wrists together with the cord. If the couple isn't friendly enough for both to be there, or if one of them is unavailable for any other reason, tie the person present to a picture of the one who isn't there. The officiant who doesn't do the tying then says:

> *The ties that bound you were strong.*

One member of the couple then cuts the cord with the knife, while the other says:

> *But even the strongest ties may break,*

The one who cut the cord holds it up while the other says:

> *Leaving their echoes behind.*

They each put their own half of the cord in the ground or bag, saying as they do:

> *May the ties dissolve,*

They then put some dirt on top of the cord and plant the seeds. This is especially important if the couple have children. As they plant the seeds, they say:

> *Nourishing what they have produced.*

The priest or priestess offers one of the couple the cup of water, saying:

> *This cup that once bound you now dissolves the binding.*

If it's not the original cup, the officiant can say:

A cup once bound you; a cup now dissolves the binding.

One of the couple pours half the water on the seeds, and the other the rest. The priest or priestess then puts the cup in the bag, ties the bag closed, and puts it on the ground. The couple take turns breaking the cup. When it's sufficiently broken, one member of the couple says:

No more will it bind.

The other says:

No more will it unbind.

The couple together fill in the hole and stamp the dirt down. If they used a bag for an indoor ritual, they pack it with their hands. The priest and priestess hold their hands out in blessing and say:

Go now, walk freely, from this place of unbinding.

The couple walk away in different directions without looking back, while the priest or priestess says:

Untie, untie
the bonds of fate
and loose the knots that held you together.
Dissolve.
Dissipate.
Disappear.
The knots pass away slowly until nothing is left
but the shape of where they once were,
ready to be filled again.

If a bag's been used, the priest or priestess will need to bury it outside later.

CHAPTER 10

Death

What happens when a Pagan dies? We've been so identified with the material world and so attached to the earth—now what?

Most Pagans believe that each person has a spiritual aspect—a soul or a spirit. Their beliefs about what exactly this is, or even how many there are, differ, but they mostly agree on its existence. And they believe that, while it is obviously connected to and affected by a material body, it survives that body's demise.

So where does it go? Most Pagans would agree that it goes to another world, variously called the Summerland, *Tír na nÓg*, the Land of Faerie, the Land of Yemos, or simply the Otherworld. The image most often employed for the passage to this spiritual realm is of a journey by water or air, either to the north, the direction of greatest darkness, or to the west, where the sun dies its daily death. The soul goes to be rested and refreshed, to relax from this world's trials, and to assimilate the lessons it has learned. It may stay in this land for a long or a short period of time (and the Otherworld's time may run at a different speed than ours anyway).

Many Pagans believe that, when ready, the soul is reborn into this world. This is our world: we live within it; we die within it; and we return to it. There may be another world between lives, but we return here to live again. After life, a death; after death, a life. Most Pagans who believe in this cycle of reincarnation would agree that we are reborn into a human body, though some accept the possibility of animal rebirth.

There are two theories of how the circumstances of rebirth are determined. One is that the soul itself decides, based on what it feels it most needs to continue its advancement toward godhood. The more common belief is that our actions in this life determine the circumstances of our next, that cause and effect operate across the borders of death. Pagans have borrowed the Hindu word *karma* to express this, believing that a soul's karma determines how it's returned to a physical body, either at conception, during gestation, or at birth.

It's also possible that we're reborn elsewhere, on other physical planets or on other spiritual planes. As a Pagan, however, I believe that I'm most likely to be reborn on this world, on my beloved earth. So where do Pagans go when they die? There's really no need for them to *go* anywhere.

Sometimes a soul doesn't accept its death, doesn't even believe it's died. This is most common with sudden deaths. When this happens, instead of being able to relax in the Otherworld, the soul tries to come back to this world. In short, it becomes a ghost. Dealing with ghosts thus consists mainly of convincing them of their death. And one of the purposes of Pagan death customs (wakes, funerals, commemorations, and Samhain) is to acknowledge the death and thereby convince the dead person of it.

That there are apparently conflicting beliefs regarding death is natural. For instance, the Romans, while believing that the dead had gone to another world, still performed rituals that implied that the dead lived on in the tomb. Moreover, this belief isn't limited to ancient times. I once heard the Christian parents of a murdered man say they were going to the cemetery to tell their son the news that his murderer had been convicted. Reincarnation, the Summerland, grave rituals, ancestor rites—these are all aspects of the complicated pattern of Paganism. They help both the living and the dead to deal with loss, and that's enough to justify them.

Modern Paganism doesn't have the same kind of comforting words some other religions do for dealing with death. We can't tell ourselves that our loved ones are now living forever in a better place, or that we will see them again when we ourselves die. We have our own ways of finding and offering comfort. We've experienced death and rebirth many times. We've followed the seasons, watching life return in the spring. We've faced death at Samhain, welcoming our ancestors and honoring death itself.

Death and rebirth, survival after death and return, aren't just beliefs to us. We know them like we know our own height. They're part of our lives, not something to be thought of just at funerals, but guides for everyday living. We belong to this world, and we will return here. We belong to our loved ones, and we will return with them. This is how Pagans comfort each other in the face of loss, with an ease born of familiarity and a knowledge born of experience.

Wakes

The word "wake" means "watch." The custom of waking thus came from the tradition of watching over a dead person. This may have had the mundane purpose of protecting them from robbers or other predators (or to make sure they were really dead before they were buried), but it's more likely intended to protect from them from bad spirits or to prevent their spirits from bothering the living.

The way the wake has evolved in the United States is as a time for family and friends to gather in a room in a funeral home. The dead person (called "the deceased") is there in his coffin (called a "casket"). People stand around wondering what they're supposed to do. At some point, there's a prayer service. Finally, everyone talks to each other about anything, as long as it has nothing to do with death or the business at hand. The whole event seems orchestrated for the purpose of denying that a death has even occurred.

This type of wake isn't all bad. It reminds us that, even in the midst of death, life goes on. It emphasizes the ties of family and friends in a time of crisis, and it begins the process of dealing with the loss. But it leaves out what should be an important part of the event. Before we can reassure ourselves that life goes on, we first need to recognize that someone has in fact died and then remember that person.

Wakes should be fairly informal, though. Different people have different needs, and those who need an informal gathering should be allowed to have one. Remember, too, that a Pagan's death affects those who are outside of the Pagan community as well. While it's common for funerals to be limited to those very close to the dead person, wakes can be attended by a large number of acquaintances, including co-workers and sometimes even friends of friends. These people need to grieve in their own way, so be sure to schedule time for both the usual socializing and a remembrance service.

Wakes as we know them in America aren't held in all cultures. In England, for example, there's no viewing of the body. Some people think the viewing is macabre, while others find it a way of convincing themselves that a loved one is really dead. Wakes can be held with either open or closed coffins, or no coffin at all. None of this is essentially Pagan, although the visible presence of the corpse is indicative of the easy relationship that Pagans cultivate between death and the world. If the body isn't visible, or perhaps not even present, a picture of the dead person can serve as the focal point for a wake. The important thing is that there must be no attempt to deny the *fact* of death. One of the purposes of wakes and funerals is to begin the process of accepting this reality.

Since a death affects an entire family, it will naturally affect the children of the family. They should be allowed to take part in wakes and funerals to the extent that they wish to. If they don't feel up to participating, or if you think they're not ready (think carefully on this), that's fine. If they want to take part, however, they shouldn't be prevented. It's a sign of maturity to do so. By taking part in these events, they're entering into the responsibilities of life, one of which is to acknowledge death. And since they have only one chance to participate, they may regret it later if they don't.

If possible, hold the wake in the home of the dead person. The household guardians and the spirits of the ancestors will be able to take part more easily if the ritual is on their home turf. From a practical point of view, this will ensure that things will be done the way you want them done. It will also convey the message that death is a part of normal life, not something to be quarantined from.

If it's not possible to have the wake at home (and it usually isn't), make sure that what you want done is possible in the funeral home you have chosen. The further in advance you can make arrangements, the better. If the funeral director is concerned that noises will disturb other wakes, see if you can find a time that doesn't conflict, or perhaps find another funeral home.

If you can't have the wake at a place where your guardians are already established, bring their images or some other objects that were significant to the dead person with you to the wake. Put them on a table, either at the foot or the head of the coffin, along with a fire and an offering bowl. If the funeral home doesn't allow lit candles, use an electric one. Light the fire and call the guardians so they can take part, and then make an offering to them. You may want to do this before non-Pagan guests arrive so you don't make them feel uncomfortable or have to explain. Leave the fire burning throughout the wake, and extinguish it after everyone has gone.

Pagan Waking Ritual

After sufficient time has passed to allow for informal socializing and the viewing of the body by those who wish to do so, have the person who's presiding call for attention with either a drum or bells, and then say:

> We are here to remember one of us who has died.
> Everyone is part of many communities
> and those of [name] are here today.
> It is time to remember [name].
> When the talking stick reaches you, tell us about [name].
> Speak from your heart of what you most know.
> If you do not wish to speak, pass the stick on.
> There is no shame in not speaking,
> only in not remembering.

Pass around a talking stick—a short, decorated stick that's passed from hand to hand to indicate who's speaking. If another object's more appropriate to the tradition of the dead, you can use that. The holder of the stick or object then speaks about the person, trying always to speak from the heart, but not so long that the others become bored. When each person is finished, the stick or object is passed to the next person.

While the stick is in someone's possession, they may not be interrupted. No one should feel obligated to speak, but neither should anyone try to take over the proceedings with a long speech. If this happens, a gentle reminder from the person presiding is not out of order.

When the stick has gone full circle, the person presiding says:

> *We have gathered and we have remembered.*
> *We have done the right thing.*
> *It is good.*

The others present say:

> *It is good.*

The person presiding then puts the stick on or in the coffin and says:

> *Our thoughts go with you.*
> *We will remember.*

The person presiding then thanks everyone for coming and invites them to stay for a while if they want to. This may be a good time for more socializing or more ritual, if it seems right.

Funerals

There is no specifically Pagan way to dispose of a dead person. Pagans have practiced cremation, burial, and exposure. Their dead have been laid to rest in stone tombs, in the earth, in water, and walled up in pyramids. Bodies have been left permanently interred, rearranged after the flesh has rotted, or removed to make room for new bodies. In fact, Pagans have used just about every way possible to dispose of the bodies of their dead. We can't look strictly to our past for guidance, then, on this subject. All these methods have a long history of Pagan use behind them, but there's nothing particularly Pagan or non-Pagan about any of them. Instead, we have to ask ourselves how a Pagan's body should be disposed of *today*.

The two main choices for the disposal of remains in our culture are burial and cremation. Neither are particularly desirable from an environmental point of view. The way bodies are usually buried prevents them from returning to the soil, and the intense heat used in crematoria (supplied by polluting energy sources) leaves very little that the earth can use. Perhaps, someday, Pagans will have cemeteries where the dead can be buried with minimum "packaging," allowing a true return to the soil. For now, however, "green" funerals, with a coffin that will rot and no embalming, are possible in some places. If you want a green funeral, check with a funeral home before it's necessary to see if the practice is available near you.

In any case, Pagans will want to rest gently in the Earth and not make their deaths the source of one more scar upon her lovely face. No large memorials, no bronze caskets, and preferably no embalming. At best, they will want their funeral rituals to involve just the body with such ritual tools and personal items that should belong to no one else. Second best is a wooden box that will soon return the body's elements to the soil. And if they're cremated, they will want their ashes returned to the earth from which they came.

Unlike wakes, funerals should be formal and ritualistic. Formality is very comforting. When everything is falling apart, structure is welcome. And no one in the midst of grief should be expected to organize a ritual or develop meaningful ways of expressing that grief. If a mourner has experienced the same form of funeral numerous times, they have the advantage of not having to think too much at a difficult time. They can run on autopilot, as it were.

I recommend that all Pagans write or adapt a funeral ritual to their own needs during their lifetime and make sure it's in the hands of a friend who can make sure it's performed upon their death. A good way to do this is to put a file on your computer and tell other people about it. Remember that there may be legal requirements for this, so consult a lawyer to make sure your wishes will be honored.

I give two funeral rituals here—one for Wiccans and one for those who practice shamanism.

Wiccan Funeral Rite

This ritual involves a descent with the dead to the Land of the Dead, with a final farewell there and an affirmation of rebirth. This is followed by a return to the world of the living. The Land of the Dead is conceived of here as a shadow realm, in many ways a mirror image of this world. Thus dark clothing and white faces and counterclockwise motion all play a role here. This isn't to say, of course, that the Otherworld is a depressing place. In this rite, the entry of the living, however, is only into its outer region, its vestibule, and that can indeed be a forbidding place, especially for the living.

The ritual is intended to be performed at the cemetery or crematorium. First, establish sacred space (see below). If possible, orient the grave so that the foot end is in the north or west, so that the dead person's journey can be seen as beginning in one of those directions. At the head end of the grave, put two chairs, one on either side of a table. On the table put a knife, a cup of water, a plate with three apple seeds, and a bowl of powdered red chalk. In ancient times, ochre was used for this, but that may be hard to find today. Instead, you can use artists' chalk and crush it into a powder. If the dead person had ancestral symbols in their shrine, or symbols of a patron deity, place them on the table as well. Put a bowl of white powder (chalk or flour) at the edge of the sacred space next to a large bowl or bottle of water, a towel, a plate with bread or crackers on it, and something to drink. You'll also need anything the dead person may have wanted buried with them.

Before the body is brought to the cemetery or crematorium, have a priest and priestess, along with an assistant to serve as Guide of Souls, go there and create sacred space. The guide will hand required objects to the participants of the ritual. The priest and priestess should wear dark clothing and do everything counterclockwise, the direction of death and dissolution. They will be calling on the God and Goddess in a form connected with death. The priestess says:

> Come, Dark Mother, come to us,
> Crone who Brings Comfort and Rest, come to us:
> Come, by the screeching Wind.
> Come, by the cleansing Fire.
> Come, by the absorbing Water.
> Come, by the restful Earth.
> Come, by the spirit that waits.
> Come to your people.
> Be with us now.

The priest then says:

> Come, Horned One, come to us.
> Stern Lord of the Land of Death, come to us.
> Come, by the chilling whirlwind.
> Come, by the force of fire.
> Come, by the receiving sea.
> Come, by the accepting Earth.
> Come, by the Spirit that waits.
> Come to your people.
> Be with us now.

The priest and priestess then sit in silence while the guide summons the other participants, who should also be dressed in dark clothing. Either the priest or the priestess may start a slow drumbeat to call the dead person home.

The nearest relative of the opposite sex to the dead person (or friend, if they have no relatives) has a cord tied around their wrist by the guide, with the other end tied to the coffin. When the relative or friend reaches the outer edge of the sacred place, the guide says:

> *We are at the edge of the Land of Death.*
> *Will you go on?*

The relative or friend says:

> *We will go on, with steadfast hearts.*

The other participants say:

> *We will go on, with steadfast hearts.*

As participants cross the border into the sacred space, the guide whitens their faces. With a large number of people, you may have to have more than one person doing this, or you can limit the whitening to a line across the forehead. Unless there's an exceptional amount of room, the coffin will have to be brought to its place by the shortest route, but the others can be brought into the sacred space along a counterclockwise spiral toward the center. As they go, the guide says:

> *We journey down into the center.*
> *We have left the land of the living behind.*

A spiral of seven circuits will bring to mind the ancient Mediterranean belief in the journey of the soul through the seven planets. If there isn't enough room for seven turns, try to make three, to represent the moon's phases and the sacred number of the Indo-Europeans. When everyone has stopped, the body is placed next to or over the grave. If there's been drumming, it stops once the coffin's been put there. The priest then gives the relative or friend a knife, who cuts the cord tied to the coffin. As they do this, the relative or friend says:

> *Everything changes.*
> *Everything passes.*
> *Go, friend, on your journey.*
> *We have come this far in love,*
> *but we can no longer walk with you.*
> *Change may not be undone;*

that which passes, passes away.
Go, now, to the land of the gods,
the Summerland, the Land of Apples,
there to rest and be refreshed.
But when you are ready to be reborn on the Earth,
may it be in the same time and the same place as your
    loved ones
that we may meet, and know, and remember, and love again.

(From "may it be" to the end is from the Gardnerian *Book of Shadows*.)

If the relative or friend is unable to say this, which is perfectly understandable under the circumstances, the words can be said by the priest or priestess, whichever is of the sex opposite to the deceased. The priestess then takes the red powder from the table and uses it to draw a sacred sign that was meaningful to the deceased (a pentagram, Thor's hammer, circle, etc.) on the dead person's forehead, saying:

Receive rebirth from my hand
when it is time, when it is time.

The relative or friend says:

Go now, marked with the sign of life,
on the way that has been taken by so many before you.

The cut cord is then put in the coffin and the coffin closed. If it's to be buried, the coffin is lowered into the ground while the priestess says:

We commit [here say all the names by which the deceased
    was known, including nicknames and sacred names] to
    your care, Mother Earth.
Love your child, cherish your child, feed your child,
Let your child grow
until he/she is ready for rebirth.

If the relative is a woman, she now pours water on the coffin. If not, another woman can do it, saying:

> *The sea is the womb*
> *from which we sprang*
> *and which absorbs us again in the end.*

If the relative is a man, he now drops three apple seeds onto the coffin. If not, another man can do it, saying:

> *The seed goes into the darkness*
> *and from it comes new life.*

If the deceased is to be cremated, this is the point in the ceremony when the body is committed to the flames. If this is the case, replace the words "Mother Earth" with "Father of Fire."

If the deceased is being buried, close relatives and friends can help fill in the grave—perhaps not completely, but each person should put in at least one handful of dirt. Although it may be painful for some, this is a healing act, an opportunity to give one last gift to their loved one, while at the same time impressing on them the finality of their loss. When this is done, the priest says:

> *He/she is with the Ancestors now,*
> *in the Land of Youth.*

The priestess says:

> *This very moment, even as we stand here in the*
> *   Land of Death,*
> *new life is being born.*
> *Perhaps even our friend is ready to be reborn.*
> *Out there, in the world we live in, life goes on.*
> *Life is good.*
> *Blessed be life!*

All say:

> *Blessed be life!*

Everyone, except the priest and priestess, spirals out again, this time in a clockwise direction. It is important that they all turn the same number of times they did coming in, so as to completely return to the land of the living. As they leave the circle, the guide or someone else wipes the white off their faces. When they have all left the circle, they turn to face the center once more. The relative or friend says:

> *You have gone to be with the Ancestors and we will*
> *remember you.*

Everyone responds, in a call-and-reponse fashion:

> *We will remember you.*

The relative or friend says:

> *On the day of remembering and all the days between,*

All respond:

> *we will remember you.*

The relative or friend says:

> *When the ocean brings us words and the wind whispers*
> *its messages,*

All respond:

> *we will remember you.*

The relative or friend says:

> *At the rising of the moon, at the coming of the sun,*

All respond:

> we will remember you.

The relative or friend says:

> In the lives we live and the ways we go,

All respond:

> we will remember you.

The relative or friend says:
> Have no doubt.
> Feel no fears.

All respond:

> We will remember you.

Everyone is then given something to eat from the plate of bread or crackers and something to drink, to mark their return. They then go to change their clothes to something more cheerful before gathering somewhere to eat and drink and talk. After the others have left, the priest and priestess recast the sacred space, this time moving clockwise, before saying farewell to the God and Goddess and banishing the space.

Shamanic Funeral Rite

This ritual is performed at the grave site, or at the spot where the ashes will be disposed of. Place a pile of stones next to the grave, one for each person attending. Depending on cemetery requirements, these can be small or large. If the cemetery won't allow stones at all, see if they'll allow pegs that can be pushed into the ground. If even pegs are unacceptable, use a container of birdseed from which each person can scatter a handful. Put apple seeds in a bowl near the grave, and provide drums or rattles for those who want them. Have the dead person's nearest relative place the deceased's drum into the grave so that the coffin will rest on top of it. In this way, the dead person may ride their drum to the land of the gods. The coffin is then lowered and the hole partially filled, to the beat of slow drumming. The drumming continues while the person presiding says:

> Our friend is dead.
> Our friend is gone.
> Our friend has set sail.
> Our friend is on his/her way.
> Go, with our blessings.
> Our drums fill your sails and speed you home
> to the Summerland, the Land of Apples.
> Go, and rest.
> And when rested, return.
> Be reborn among friends.
> Be reborn among your people.

The nearest relative then throws some apple seeds into the grave and each person picks up a marker (a stone, a peg, or a handful of birdseed) and lays it down around the grave so that, together, they form the shape of a ship. This is also the shape of a vagina. Thus the ship that carries the dead person away is also the path through which they'll be reborn.

The participants can lay the stones down in silence or say a goodbye as they do so. It must be understood by all, however, that the choice between remaining silent or speaking is theirs. If some would like to say something, but don't know what, they can say:

> One last thing I do for you as you go on your way.

Or simply:

> Goodbye, [name].

When all the markers are placed, the person presiding says:

Goodbye, goodbye.
Go on your way.
You go your way, and we go ours.
We will remember you.

The others repeat the words "we will remember you," and then they leave the cemetery without looking back. The drumming stops when they're far enough away.

After either of these rituals, participants should go to someone's house to socialize further. The living have their own needs too. Be sure to call out the deceased's name at the next Samhain.

Commemoration

There's a custom among some peoples, particularly well-known among Jews, of commemorating the anniversary of a relative's death. The Yiddish name for this celebration is *Yahrzeit,* the "year-time." The observance fulfills several functions, but one of the more important is to allow for a socially sanctioned time of mourning that has a distinct end. Although mourning is a personal thing and the length of time needed for it varies from person to person, sometimes people feel guilty about ending their grieving. An official day on which it's considered okay to stop mourning can be a great help to them.

Among Pagans, commemorations are frequently held a year and a day after a death. This allows for a whole year to pass before moving on to a new phase of life. A commemoration ritual therefore acknowledges that a period of change is over and a new time is beginning.

At the beginning of a commemoration, light a candle that will burn for the whole period. (Yahrzeit candles, candles in a jar that burn for a long time, can be found in many grocery stores.) As you light the candle, say:

You are with us now.
We have not forgotten you.

Spend the day fasting, meditating, and remembering. Friends may wish to stop by and remember with close relatives. At the very end of the day, visit the cemetery. Perform the acts of remembrance performed at Samhain (see chapter 8) and leave without looking back. Return to the home of the family of the dead person, or to that of a close relative or friend, and have a meal.

Alternatively, if people consider that their mourning has reached an appropriate stopping point by the Samhain after the funeral, you can hold these observances then. Whenever they're held, though, make sure you remember the deceased at Samhain. It's especially important to call out the names of the dead at the first Samhain after their death. Remember them.

Afterword

Children are born to the People. We welcome them and bless them, teach them and celebrate with them. When they come of age, we honor them and send them on their way with our blessings to find lives of their own and continue the work. And then we ourselves someday die, leaving them behind in our place.

It is good that things should be this way. We live, we raise children, we die. And we are reborn. And so the Wheel turns. It is indeed good. The world is indeed good, and all its ways are good. We who call ourselves Pagans say this, that the world is good.

May our children be blessed. May our children bless us. May all who read these words be blessed, and may you pass this blessing on and on, handing the old ways down, for as long as earth and sky endure.

Protective Symbols

These symbols can be painted or carved over doors and windows, or drawn on them with oil or water during house blessings. They can also be painted, carved, or burned on pieces of wood and worn around the neck as amulets, or drawn on someone's forehead with a finger, either with or without oil or water as part of a blessing. Finally, they can be put on a crib to extend protection over a baby.

Symbol	How Made	Meaning
		Pentagram, represents the four elements, plus spirit, bound together.
		Moon, invokes the protection of the Goddess.
		Triple Goddess, represented by three dots.
		Equal-armed cross, represents the four directions, the elements, sky and earth, the sacred and the profane. Used by both Pagans and Christians, and thus especially useful in interfaith families.

Symbol	How Made	Meaning
		Thor's hammer, symbol of the great Norse protector of the common people.
		Circle, represents wholeness and completeness, and thus a barrier against external forces.
		Twin-bladed axe, both a God and Goddess symbol. Called a labrys when used as a Goddess symbol. It's one of the common emblems of the supposed matriarchal culture of ancient Crete. It is also the typical weapon of the Indo-European thunder and warrior god.
		Dolmen, Neolithic portal between our world and the world of the gods. It therefore provides an opening for sacred influence and protection.

Appendix B:
Sacred Offerings

Different types of spiritual entities prefer different types of offerings. If you're working with a particular named deity or spirit, research just what that deity prefers. These lists are intended only as a good start and can be especially useful when working with unnamed spirits.

Types of Spiritual Being	Food	Drink	Incense	Other
Nature Spirits	cornmeal, grain, fruit, cheese	beer	sage, tobacco	quartz, pebbles, shiny objects
House Spirits	bread, salt, butter, oil, fruit	milk, wine, beer	frankincense, rosemary	
Border Guardians	eggs, honey, cakes	milk, wine, beer	rosemary, thyme, juniper	flower garlands
Hearth Guardians	bread, butter, oil	milk	pine, rosemary	
Threshold Guardians	barley, bread	wine	juniper	

Types of Spiritual Being	Food	Drink	Incense	Other
Garden Spirits	bread, fruit, cornmeal	milk	bay	flowers
Deities in General	bread	wine, beer, milk	frankincense	
Birth Goddesses	bread, eggs, cookies	milk	sandalwood, mint, rose	infant's hair, umbilical cord
Ancestors	beans, caraway, food and drink from the family table	dark beer		hair

Appendix C:
Ritual Colors

Ritual gains force when symbols reinforce each other, for instance, the offerings appropriate to a deity with words that suit them. One kind of symbol is color. These can be used in decorations, clothing, jewelry, or anything else you use in a ritual.

Samhain: black

Yule: red, green, white, gold

Imbolc: red, green

Ostara: yellow, pastels

May Day: green, multicolored

Midsummer: yellow, rainbow

Lammas: gold

Harvest: yellow, orange, red, purple, colors of fall leaves and twilight

Full or waxing moon: white, silver, light blue

Dark moon: black, dark blue

Sources and Resources

These are references I found useful in preparing this book, combined with suggestions for more that you may find useful. Don't neglect books on general parenting; non-Pagans have some good advice on raising happy and healthy children too. And, after all, that's what we most want.

Books and Articles

Ashcroft-Nowicki, Dolores. *First Steps in Ritual*. Ritual theory, with rituals for a variety of occasions. Includes ritual for attracting a Slavic house spirit, and a Chinese ritual for honoring the god of the stove.

Brand, John. *Observations on the Popular Antiquities of Great Britain*. Originally published in 1848, this is a gold mine of information. Gives customs for seasonal celebrations, birth, handfasting, betrothals, funerals, and much more.

Campanelli, Pauline. *Ancient Ways: Reclaiming Pagan Traditions*.

——————. *Wheel of the Year: Living the Magical Life*. Both books give folk traditions and rituals for seasonal observances, and both are excellent sources for family observances.

Carmichael, Alexander. *Carmina Gadelica*. Prayers and songs collected in the Hebrides around the turn of the century. Some made their way into the Gardnerian *Book of Shadows*. Magnificent.

Carroll, David. *Spiritual Parenting*. Advice on child rearing from a New Age point of view. Includes tips on teaching meditation to children.

Cross, Tom P., and Clark Harris Slover. *Ancient Irish Tales.* A large collection of the more important medieval Irish stories. A bit advanced, but they can be reworked for children.

Cunningham, Scott. *The Magical Household.* Concerned more with the craft of Wicca than the religion. It has good sections on the seasons, gardens, altars, and household protection.

——————. *Wicca: A Guide for the Solitary Practitioner.* Although concerned mainly with those who work alone, many of this book's rituals can work with children.

Danaher, Kevin. *The Year in Ireland.* Seasonal customs in Ireland. Belongs in every Celtophile's library.

Dangler, Michael J. *The Fire on Our Hearth: A Devotional of Three Cranes Grove, ADF.* A collection of prayers and short rituals in a variety of Indo-European traditions.

DeGidio, Sandra. *Enriching Faith through Family Celebrations.* A Christian treatment of many of the themes discussed in this book, giving many good suggestions, particularly on seasonal celebrations.

Della Volpe, Angel. "From the Hearth to the Creation of Boundaries," *Journal of Indo-European Studies* 18: 1 & 2, (1990), pp. 157–84. Information primarily on hearths, but also sacred space, weddings, and births.

Dexter, Miriam Robbins. *Whence the Goddesses: A Source Book.* Essentially an expansion and popularization of her dissertation, this is the best book on goddesses I've found.

Dues, Greg. *Catholic Customs and Traditions: A Popular Guide.* This book mistakenly identifies Samhain with a Celtic god of the dead, but has some good ideas, especially of what Neo-Paganism is missing out on but could incorporate.

Farrar, Janet, and Stewart Farrar. *Eight Sabbats for Witches*. A lot of information on seasonal customs and beliefs, baby blessing, handfasting, and funerals. Relies a bit too heavily on Frazer's *The Golden Bough* and Graves's *The White Goddess* for my taste, but still good.

Farrar, Stewart. *What Witches Do*.

Fitch, Ed. *Magical Rites from the Crystal Well*. Includes seasonal rituals, baby blessings, handfasting, divorce, and funerals.

——————. *The Rites of Odin*. Norse Neo-Pagans have done well integrating their religions and their families. Contains seasonal rituals, betrothals, weddings, birth-pledging, coming of age, divorce, and funerals. Horrific from the point of view of representing actual Norse practice, though; it's essentially Wicca with Norse names, but the rituals are still nice.

Fitzpatrick, Jean Grasso. *Something More: Nurturing Your Child's Spiritual Growth*. Mostly Judeo-Christian, but still useful.

Ford, Patrick K. (ed. and tr.). *The Mabinogi and Other Medieval Welsh Tales*. You'll need to retell them, but these are great medieval Welsh stories that may preserve elements of Pagan myths.

Frazer, Sir James (Theodor Gaster, editor). *The New Golden Bough*. Although Frazer's conclusions have been rejected by anthropology, and even some of his data have been shown to be shaky, this is still a good source for folk customs.

Fulghum, Robert. *From Beginning to End: The Rituals of Our Lives*. Ritual theory and examples for modern times, from a Unitarian minister.

Gantz, Jeffrey (tr.). *Early Irish Myths and Sagas*.

Gaster, Theodor H. *Festivals of the Jewish Year*. In discussing the traditions of Jewish celebrations, he gives many customs from other traditions.

Gonda, J. *Vedic Ritual: The Non-Solemn Rites*. I hesitated to include this because it's expensive and hard to find, but it contains many ideas for family rituals in the Vedic tradition. I found my copy at a university library.

Green, Marian. *A Calendar of Festivals: Traditional Celebrations, Songs, Seasonal Recipes, and Things to Make.* Wonderful suggestions for seasonal observances. Two warnings, however. First, the recipes are written for a British audience and may need some translation. She writes "jelly" where Americans would say "gelatin," for instance. Second, while her reporting of ancient customs is generally spot on, the explanations and etymologies she gives for them are frequently in error or are speculation rather than fact. Used carefully, this is a welcome addition to anyone's library.

Gundarsson, Kveldulf. *Teutonic Religion: Folk Beliefs and Practices of the Northern Tradition.* Mostly useful in this context for calendar festivals and rituals that can be adapted for the family.

Hutton, Ronald. *The Stations of the Sun.* Folk customs for calendar celebrations in Britain.

James, Edwin Oliver. *Seasonal Feasts and Festivals.* Prehistoric, Egyptian, Mesopotamian, Palestinian, Anatolian, Greek, Roman, and European Christian seasonal celebrations.

Leach, Maria (ed.). *Funk & Wagnalls Standard Dictionary of Folklore, Mythology, and Legend.* A must for anyone interested in folk customs.

MacNeill, Maire. "The Musician in the Cave," *Béaloideas* 57 (1989), pp. 109–32. A treatment of Lugnasad customs and folklore.

McCarroll, Tolbert. *Guiding God's Children.* Written from the point of view of a Christian monk. Strongly influenced by Zen Buddhism, the emphasis is on spirituality and nature.

McNeill, F. Marian. *The Silver Bough* (4 vols.). Folk customs from Scotland.

Mitchell, Stephen (tr.). *Gilgamesh.* The oldest novel. Great story, with lots of meaning. You'll probably have to retell it, but it's worth it.

Newall, Venetia. "Easter Eggs," *Journal of American Folklore* 80 (1967), pp. 3–32. Not just about Easter and not just America; egg myths and customs from around the world associated with birth, weddings, funerals, May Day, Harvest, and planting.

Newmann, Dana. *The Complete Teacher's Almanack: A Daily Guide to All Twelve Months of the Year*. Seasonal, holiday, environmental, and Native American activities for young children.

Ono, Sokyo. *Shinto: The Kami Way*. Shinto, the folk religion of Japan, is the only form of Paganism that has survived to this day in an industrialized culture, and it thus has a lot to teach us. It's especially useful in researching household shrines, offerings, and ancestor worship.

Orr, David G. "Roman Domestic Religion: The Evidence of the Household Shrines," *Aufstieg und Niedergang der Römischen Welt II* 16:2 (1978), pp. 1557–1591.

Ovid. *Fasti*. A poem describing the first half of the Roman year.

——. *The Metamorphoses*. A collection of Roman stories, some based on Greek myths and lore.

Palmer, Susan J., and Charlotte E. Hardman, eds. *Children in New Religions*. Covers a number of religious movements, including Paganism, but there's good information in all the articles.

Plutarch. *The Roman Questions of Plutarch*.

Polome, Edgar C. "Germanic Religion and the Indo-European Heritage," *Mankind Quarterly* 26:1 & 2 (Fall/Winter, 1985), pp. 27–55.

Redford, Donald B. *The Ancient Gods Speak: A Guide to Egyptian Religion*. Gods, rituals, and beliefs.

Rig Veda. tr. and ed. Wendy Doniger O'Flaherty. Harmondsworth, UK: Penguin Books, 1981. Only a portion of this wonderful work, but a version nonetheless. A collection of truly Pagan prayers.

Roberts, Elizabeth, and Elias Amidon. *Earth Prayers from Around the World*. A collection of Pagan-friendly prayers for various occasions.

Rose, H. J. *Ancient Roman Religion*.

Serith, Ceisiwr. *The Big Book of Pagan Prayer and Ritual*.

Starhawk (Miriam Simos), Diane Baker, and Anne Hill. *Circle Round: Raising Children in Goddess Traditions*.

Syme, Daniel B. *The Jewish Home*. Especially useful for Judeo-Pagans, but can be used by anyone looking for living traditions.

Tufnell, Blanche O. "Czecho-Slovak Folklore," *Folklore* 35 (1924), pp. 26–56.

——————. "On Indo-European Ceremonial and Socio-Political Elements Underlying the Origin of Formal Boundaries," *Journal of Indo-European Studies* 20: 1 & 2 (Sp/Su, 1992), pp. 71–122. Packed with information on the domestic cults of the various Indo-European peoples. Don't let the title scare you.

Wolfe, Amber. *In the Shadow of the Shaman*. Contains exercises for awakening awareness of the spiritual side of nature.

Children's Books

These are books that can be read either by or to children. Their appropriateness will vary with the age of the child. If the book's written in a quite challenging style, it can often be simplified as it's read. I read *The Wind in the Willows* to my daughter when she was quite young; when she was older, she read it on her own and asked: "Daddy, did you change some of the words when you read this to me?" The same is true of many of the other books here as well. Have a look at them first to decide whether your child is ready for them.

Alexander, Heather. *A Child's Introduction to Greek Mythology: The Stories of the Gods, Goddesses, Heroes, Monsters, and Other Mythical Creatures*. Dinobit Publishing.

——————. *Norse Mythology: History for Kids*. A captivating guide to Norse folklore including fairy tales, legends, sagas, and myths of the Norse gods and heroes.

Earthworks Group. *Fifty Simple Things Kids Can Do to Save the Earth*. The title says it all.

Evslin, Bernard, Dorothy Evslin, and Ned Hoopes. *The Greek Gods*. The first book on mythology that I read as a kid.

Frost, Robert. "Stopping by Woods on a Snowy Evening." This poem is available in a number of editions and anthologies, as well as online. It may be interpreted as taking place on Yule, with the narrator representing the sun stopping in the darkness before continuing on his way. A reading of this poem is a Yule tradition in my family; it's one of my daughter's favorite poems (she has it memorized).

Goble, Paul. *The Gift of the Sacred Dog*. Plains Indian story of the coming of the horse.

Grahame, Kenneth. *The Wind in the Willows*. Available in a number of editions. The language is a bit difficult, so a child will have to be nine or older to read it themselves. Of special interest is chapter 7, "The Piper at the Gates of Dawn," an encounter with Pan.

Grimm, Jacob, and Wilhelm Grimm. *Fairy Tales*. Available in a number of editions. The age at which these are appropriate will vary with the child, so you will need to read them first. If you know some of these from the Disney versions, you'll find that the originals are a little more violent (one might even say "grim") than you expect.

Hallinan, P. K. *For the Love of Our Earth*. A poem designed to inspire children to care for the earth and each other.

Hamilton, Edith. *Mythology: Timeless Tales of Gods and Heroes*. Mostly Graeco-Roman, but with Norse entries toward the end.

Hartman, Jennifer. *Old Mother Frost*. Frau Holle wakes for Yule to bring happiness to children.

Hoena, Blake. *National Geographic Kids Everything Mythology: Begin Your Quest for Facts, Photos, and Fun Fit for Gods and Goddesses.*

Lionni, Leo. *Frederick.* The tale of a storytelling mouse.

Mayer, Marianna. *Noble-Hearted Kate.* An original tale, based on Celtic folklore, of Kate, who saves both her stepsister and a prince on Samhain Eve "when the veil between the realm of Faerie and the realm of man is drawn apart and anything can happen."

Moroney, Morgan E. *Gods and Goddesses of Ancient Egypt: Egyptian Mythology for Kids.*

Parramon, J. M. *The Four Elements.* A set of four books, sometimes sold separately, describing the elements.

Phelps, Ethel Johnston. Feminist Folk Tales from Around the World (4 vols.). Fairy tales in which the hero is female. Different tales are appropriate for different ages.

Pinard, Chris. *Celtic Mythology for Kids: Tales of Selkies, Giants, and the Sea.*

Sabuda, Robert. *Winter's Tale.* Pop-up book in which animals appear throughout winter before he goes away.

Tresselt, Alvin, and Henri Sorensen. *The Gift of the Tree.* The story of an oak tree's rotting and the gift of life it gives to the forest.

Wood, Audrey. *When the Root Children Wake Up.* Land spirits sing and dance through summer, until winter comes.

Wood, Douglas. *Grandad's Prayers of the Earth.* A boy's grandfather teaches him about the prayers of the trees.

Zeman, Ludila. *Gilgamesh the King; The Revenge of Ishtar; The Last Quest of Gilgamesh* (The Gilgamesh Trilogy).

Websites

Global Lithuanian Net. *lithuanian.net.* Mythology and some information on seasonal festivals.

Gundarsson, Kvedúlf. "Redes for Weddings." *hrafnar.org.* Advice regarding weddings. Intended for Germanic ceremonies, but relevant to other Pagan traditions.

Moons, Moody. "Handfasting and How to Handle Your Non-Pagan Family." *moodymoons.com.*

"What It's Like Being a Modern Pagan Family." *yourtango.com.*

Music

Corrigan, Ian. *Once Around the Wheel: Modern and Traditional Seasonal Songs.* Cleveland Heights, Ohio: Association for Consciousness Exploration, 1987. Recorded at a workshop. Includes seasonal songs and discussion of customs.

EarthSpirit Community. *This Winter's Night. earthspirit.com.* Songs for Yule.

Kennedy, Peter, and Alan Lomax (editors). *Folk Songs of Britain, Vol. IX: Songs of Ceremony* (on vinyl). Seasonal songs, including May carols, John Barleycorn, and Wassailing songs.

Macha, Michaela. "Norse Mythology and Asatru Poetry and Music." *odins-gift.com.* Lots of songs. Many (especially those for Yule) are, unfortunately, written to pre-existing tunes.

Pendderwen, Gwydion. *Songs for the Old Religion.* Pagan songs, mostly seasonal.

YouTube Channels and Videos

YouTube has a lot of videos with songs, pictures of altars and shrines, and rituals suitable or adaptable for families.

Ceisiwr Serith. My own channel has songs, rituals, and pictures of shrines.

The Flirtations. "Breaths." Originally by Sweet Honey in the Rock, but I really like this version.

Immaruka Lillacmess. Contains two lovely songs by Anne Hill: "Circle Round" and "Persephone."

Kellianna Music. A large number of songs, some appropriate for seasonal festivals, and some wonderful ones to particular deities. I'm particularly fond of "This New Day," a Pagan song with a bluesy rather than pseudo-Celtic sound. Very refreshing.

Sarah Pirtle. "Two Hands Hold the Earth." Some of the songs can be connected with Paganism; some are just fun.

S. J. Tucker. "Solstice Night." Simply delightful.

Skaldic Hearth Kin. "Winter Wassail" Playlist of Pagan songs. Some have a Norse twist, but most are generally Pagan.

Wyrd Sisters. "Solstice Carole."

About the Author

Ceisiwr Serith (David Fickett-Wilbar) is a writer and teacher in the Pagan community. His interest in prayers and rituals grew naturally as a result of his work in the Wiccan and Druidic traditions. He melded this work with the most important part of his life, as a husband and father; *A Book of Pagan Family Prayers and Rituals* is a result. Ceisiwr is also the author of *A Book of Pagan Prayer, The Big Book of Pagan Prayer and Ritual,* and *Deep Ancestors: Practicing the Religion of the Proto-Indo-Europeans.* His work has also been published in the *Journal of Indo-European Studies* and *Proceedings of the Harvard Celtic Colloquium.* He is a member of Ár nDraíocht Féin, a Druid fellowship, and is priest and liturgist for Nemos Ognios grove in Durham, New Hampshire.

To Our Readers

Weiser Books, an imprint of Red Wheel/Weiser, publishes books across the entire spectrum of occult, esoteric, speculative, and New Age subjects. Our mission is to publish quality books that will make a difference in people's lives without advocating any one particular path or field of study. We value the integrity, originality, and depth of knowledge of our authors.

Our readers are our most important resource, and we appreciate your input, suggestions, and ideas about what you would like to see published.

Visit our website at *www.redwheelweiser.com*, where you can learn about our upcoming books and free downloads, and also find links to sign up for our newsletter and exclusive offers.

You can also contact us at *info@rwwbooks.com* or at

Red Wheel/Weiser, LLC
65 Parker Street, Suite 7
Newburyport, MA 01950